A BONSAI TREE

AN AUTOBIOGRAPHY

Narendra Luther

NIYOGI
BOOKS

Published by

NIYOGI BOOKS

Block D, Building No. 77,
Okhla Industrial Area, Phase-I,
New Delhi-110 020, INDIA
Tel: 91-11-26816301, 26818960
Email: niyogibooks@gmail.com
Website: www.niyogibooksindia.com

Editor: Sucharita Ghosh
Design: Shraboni Roy

ISBN: 978-81-933935-6-7
Publication: 2017

Printed at: Niyogi Offset Pvt. Ltd., New Delhi, India

To my ancestral village

Budha Goraya, now in Pakistan, where it all began –

and which I have visited only once

in my childhood

This is a fascinating story of a civil servant, a thinker and a writer. Narendra's narrative skill is superb and brings past events alive with a sense of intimacy. Though meant to be an autobiography, it is truly a commentary on India's journey from Partition and Independence to the present day. His philosophical musings on many aspects of life are insightful and comforting.

Dr C. Rangarajan
Formerly Chairman, Economic Advisory Council to the Prime Minster,
Former Governor, RBI & Chairman, Madras School of Economics

A searingly honest and deeply felt story.

Writing so simply and openly about the life-changing experiences of the author and his family show immense strength of character.

Since I was born and grew up in Hyderabad, there is a warm familiarity and recognition of both time and place during which some of the events mentioned in the book took place.

Shyam Benegal
Filmmaker

An eminently readable chronicle of the life and times of a brilliant and liberal-minded bureaucrat-turned-author. Absorbing anecdotes from his career encompass the history of the IAS. The heartrending story of the horrors of Partition experienced by Narendra makes this book truly remarkable. He offers amazing insights into the unique history and culture of Hyderabad. Surprisingly candid revelations describing the tribulations within his own family life lend a sense of pathos and gravitas to an otherwise entertaining read.

Anjolie Ela Menon
Renowned painter and sculptor

Narendra Luther's prose combines the passion of a Punjabi refugee and the wit of a Hyderabadi raconteur. Many who have enjoyed his books on Hyderabad and Hyderabadis will devour this delightful yet poignant account of his life and times.

Sanjaya Baru
Former chief editor of the *Financial Express* and the *Business Standard.*
Author of *The Accidental Prime Minster*

I have been a witness to the author's achievements as an innovative administrator, a renowned humourist and an acknowledged authority on the history and culture of Hyderabad for half a century.

Here he tells his unknown story – from the halcyon days of the Raj through the bloodbath of the Partition, followed by an unremitting struggle for survival – and success – and the agony of a secret epic battle.

This riveting story will entertain and inspire readers across generations.

Potturi Venkateswara Rao
Former editor of *Andhra Prabha* daily
Former chairman Andhra Pradesh Press Academy

CONTENTS

Age of Innocence

Just as I had a father, my father too had a father. I have seen him. I do not know my ancestors beyond that because my family tree was left behind in Pakistan in 1947. If things had remained normal, I could have traced my family tree down to Alexander's invasion. But now, I have to content myself with a truncated tree with withered roots.

As a coal dealer in a village, my paternal grandfather was always in spotless white. He achieved this miracle by merely neglecting his business. The compensation was that he became the *safed posh* – the white-clad front man of the village Budha Goraya in Sialkot district, now in Pakistan. He received every important man visiting the village and spoke on behalf of the village. I have seen his dog-eared testimonial book full of glowing tributes from visiting officials. In that he was mentioned as Kirpa Ram Ludher. My father explained that 'Ludher' was an inherited nickname of an ancestor of his. It is the Punjabi term for a small mammal with webbed feet called 'otter' in English. It lives in water and eats fish. You may have seen it in some zoo. It keeps constantly diving from one side of the pool of water to the other and back. There was a canal named *Aik* flowing by the village. The ancestor in question was so fond of swimming that he was always seen in the Aik. He was therefore nicknamed 'Ludher'. Some young man in my father's generation, embarrassed by such a surname, replaced the letter 'd' with 't' and it became Luther. I visited the village only once for a wedding when I was about nine years old.

Many persons including some of my close friends have taken me to be a Christian. This belated clarification will hopefully ensure that I die as a Hindu – the faith in which I was born.

My father, Mela Ram, was born in 1898. He was the first in his generation to break the mould of rural non-agricultural poverty. He used to trudge miles to go to school and ultimately completed his graduation with honours first class first. To that he added a degree in teaching from Patiala. Such a bright young man in the community was a hot commodity and he was picked up by my maternal grandfather as a match for his daughter while he was still to pass his finals. My mother used to tell us how she, an urban girl from Lahore, was suddenly taken to a village and for some time had to adjust to living in a large joint family with her in-laws.

My father was cheated out of a medical career in the army because the family could not muster enough money to pay to the recruiting officer during the First World War. For the provincial civil service, even the application form was not given to him. However, because of his brilliant academic record, he was appointed directly as headmaster of the D.A.V. High School in Dasuya in Hoshiarpur district. However, the lure of a government job was such that after sometime he left that job and joined as a lecturer in the government intermediate college in Hoshiarpur.

He inherited considerable debt and my parents were expected to discharge it for the sake of the family honour. In order to do so, my mother used to borrow interest-free loans from her parents to pay off large instalments to reduce accumulation of interest. My father was not only the eldest son, but also the eldest in his generation in the community. As such he had to undertake the education and marriage of all his siblings and even cousins. Our house was always full of young men, distant relatives from our village, who were sent by their parents to our house for education, with free board and lodging.

My mother, Lila Vati, was born about 1903 in a well-off family of Lahore, now in Pakistan. Her father, Kripa Sagar, retired as the chief accounts officer of the Punjab University, Lahore. He was a poet and playwright in Punjabi, and a celebrity in literary circles. I remember my mother once took me to a *kavi sammelan* – a large public gathering where well-known Punjabi poets were reciting their poems. My maternal grandfather, during his recitation, fumbled for some words in one of his popular poems. Thereupon my mother prompted him from where we were sitting amongst the audience. After two such promptings, my grandfather said, 'Lila, come and sit by my side instead of prompting from so far away.' My mother felt very proud at such an honour and because of the cheers of the audience. I was too small to understand anything except the clapping part in which I too joined.

He was reckoned as one of the important literary figures responsible for the revival of the Punjabi language and was a leading humorist in Punjabi prose, poetry and drama. Some of his books were prescribed for the graduation course in the university even after the Partition of the Punjab. His house was called 'Punjabi Sahitya Ghar'. There was a printing press on the ground floor of his house in Ram Gali of Lahore. He must have earned good royalties because he built a *kothi*—a bungalow—in the suburbs on Infantry Road near the cantonment. We stayed there for some years before Independence.

My mother was a tall, beautiful and high-minded woman. Raised as a favourite of her father, she was the only surviving sister of three brothers. She was somewhat domineering in her outlook. Everyone in the extended family was in awe of her. She would announce decisions and everybody had to fall in line. However, she mellowed with age in that respect. As a mother she was a disciplinarian and inculcated high ideals in her children and brought us up to believe that nothing was impossible to achieve if we worked hard enough.

Rationing was introduced at the outbreak of the Second World War in 1939 and it continued till around the Partition in 1947. Everything from flour, sugar, kerosene to fine cloth was rationed. My mother told us that we had to manage within the ration quota. She would not buy anything from the black market. When, for example, the rationed quota of sugar was exhausted, she asked us either to drink milk and tea without sugar or with *shakkar* (powder of unrefined jaggery). We did not like that because it gave the milk a muddied look. Thereupon she suggested that we put a piece of *gur* (lump of molasses) in our mouth and then drink milk so that we got a slow release of sweetness without having to suffer the sight of muddied milk. Alongside, she was quietly saving from the quota of fine cloth for my sister's dowry. Boys' knickers were stitched from new clothing made of rough grey cloth. Fortunately, our schools did not mandate any uniforms.

She would narrate stories from the *Ramayana* and the *Mahabharata* and recite slokas from the Gita to us children. Her recitation of the *dohas* from the *Tulsi Ramayana* was very impressive and became interesting when she explained their meaning to us.

She always stood out in any company and had immense zest for life and was always ready for picnics and outings. She would play badminton with us and taught us indoor games like cards, carom and chess, and play hide-and-seek with us and even with our children right up to a ripe old age. She enjoyed a good appetite but did not bother about her figure. Despite that, she maintained the same figure and weight as she had at the time of her marriage right through her life of about eighty-seven years.

Ambitious by nature her curiosity was immense. That extended to religion and metaphysics. An eternal seeker, she tried out various religious sects, like the Arya Samaj, Sikhism, Radha Soami, Sahaj Marg, Rama Krishna Mission, and finally became a Brahma Kumari. This sect has its headquarters at Mount Abu in Rajasthan. She had a missionary's zeal to spread her current fad. As a Brahma Kumari she would receive a cyclostyled copy of the daily sermon by the head of the sect. It was called 'Shiv Baba's *Murli*' – flute. She would read it very devoutly and insisted on us listening to it. After a few such inflictions, we requested to be spared from that obligation. This sect emphasized celibacy to the extent that she would not eat anything cooked by a married woman. She also refused to eat with us at the dining table if any meat dish was on the table. I was a vegetarian but my wife Bindi was not. More than that, the children wanted to eat meat occasionally. That created problems in the household of whichever son she happened to be staying with. Once on her persistence, I gave her a room to serve as a separate kitchen for her. Soon she started missing the fun of eating together, and so relented about her strict, impractical taboo.

My father was a mild-mannered person whose over-consideration of others led him to utter self-abnegation. He never demanded anything for himself. The result was that everybody wanted to have him around and to do something for him.

He was a man of Sufi outlook who used to pay regular visits to the shrine of Miyan Mir which was quite close to our house in Lahore. He read widely and took a great deal of notes. He used to translate the *ayat*s of the Quran and *sloka*s from the Gita and explain their contents to us which went over our young heads. He was what today would be called an inter-faith scholar. However, he did not share our mother's missionary zeal to improve other people. He went quietly along with my mother on her spiritual quest. However, he helped her out by explaining some of the finer points of various religions. He was a social reformist in his own way and banned *purdah* by women and did not allow them to touch his feet by way of respect. He also encouraged my mother not to bother about fasting on religious occasions. Because of his sound knowledge of Arabic and Persian, and a liberal outlook, his Muslim friends called him 'Mahatma', while Hindus – including his relatives – often referred to him as 'Maulana', half respectful and half taunting. He translated three plays of Shakespeare into Punjabi. One was taken away by Balwant Gargi for publication and misplaced by him.

The atmosphere in our house was academic, liberal, and secular. I remember a blind man from our ancestral village who regularly visited us for about a fortnight once a year. He was the *imam* from our village and knew the whole Quran by heart. He was therefore addressed as Hafiz*ji*. We were asked to be especially solicitous to him and help him go wherever he wanted. At the end of his stay, he was seen off with a gift of a set of clothes including a turban, dry fruits and some cash. For a long time, we thought every blind Muslim was called Hafiz.

*

I was born in Hoshiarpur in 1932. My father was a lecturer/teacher most of his life and retired as a district inspector of schools. Since he was in government service, he was transferred to various places. My earliest memories begin with Shimla where we spent the first seven years of my life. At that time Shimla was the summer capital of the governments of both India and the Punjab. The town was therefore kept spic and span. Only cars of the viceroy, the governor and the deputy commissioner of Shimla were allowed to ply on the Mall Road. Women who did not want to walk hired dainty rickshaws pulled by two men in uniforms. Men and children had the additional option of taking ponies. My mother would oblige me by taking a rickshaw so I could ride alongside her on a pony as her 'husband'. Since no cattle were allowed within the municipal limits, I never saw any cow or buffalo. My mother used to dress us in smart double-breasted jackets and grey knickers made of English wool and whenever we visited our relatives in Lahore during the winter vacations, our cousins were very impressed by how well turned out we were. My memories of Shimla cover a neat bungalow in which we stayed. It was fronted by what appeared to my child's eyes a huge grassy ground where we played football matches. We had to climb a steep road to reach Cart Road and thence the Mall. When I returned to Shimla in my youth, I was surprised to note the difference in the scale of vision of children and grown-ups.

An incident which stands out in my mind is when my mother took to bed and my elder sister and I were pushed out of her bedroom and asked to go out and play. We were intrigued by the unusual hush hush but there seemed to be no anxiety or concern associated with her usual bouts of illness. When we returned after an hour or so, a *dai* emerged from the room and asked us in to see what she had brought for us. We were surprised to see a baby in my mother's lap and we touched him gingerly. That was my younger brother and, considering the age difference between us, I must have been two-and-a-half at that time.

After Shimla we lived for a long time in Dharam Pura, a suburb of Lahore. The first time I saw cow dung on a road in Lahore, I was so scandalized that I rushed to my mother to report that someone had eased himself in the middle of the road! Again, when the family was discussing the purchase of a buffalo for milk, I blurted out my suggestion to buy a bullock 'because you can see it is full of white milk'. These two innocent observations of mine became jokes for three generations.

I did my primary schooling in the local school at Dharam Pura and being very shy I often suffered ragging at the hands of the senior boys.

My father did not observe any religious rituals. So we did not have the naming ceremony when the boys' heads are shaved. We did not have the thread ceremony for boys at the age of seven. We did not keep a *choti* – a tuft of hair at the back of the head – which every Hindu boy had. In class VIII, there was an examination for religious instruction carrying fifty marks. I scored full marks in the written examination.

The final stage was an oral test by two external examiners. They asked me a number of questions and I answered them satisfactorily. Finally, one of them asked me if I was Hindu. I replied in the affirmative. Thereupon, he asked me agitatedly, 'Then where is your choti?'

I replied that I did not keep one.

'Five marks deducted for that,' he declared.

At home everyone had a hearty laugh when I narrated my sad story. My father was enraged. He took up the matter with the headmaster the next day and had my marks restored.

Incidentally, this was the very topic with which I started my creative writing endeavours.

The medium of instruction was Urdu though Hindi was also taught as a subject. Urdu was also the official language of the state. During those days it was common that all males read Urdu. Amongst females, Muslims read Urdu. Hindus read Hindi and Sikhs read Gurumukhi. So strong was the association between Urdu and masculinity in our minds that when a young boy who only knew Hindi joined our class, the whole class started teasing him that he was a girl in disguise. Some boys even tried to grope him. They were stopped from doing that after the class teacher caned them.

Another strange practice in the Punjab was that while everyone spoke Punjabi, people usually adopted Urdu for official or even slightly formal occasions. Officers mostly spoke in Urdu to their subordinates. Many years later, in 2005, when I revisited Lahore, the department of Language and Culture of the Punjab government organized a reception in my honour to which writers and poets and journalists were invited. Everyone spoke in Punjabi. When my turn came to respond to the felicitations, I said I had never made a speech in Punjabi. They asked me to not bother and speak in Urdu instead. We were the guests of Sayed Babar Ali, a prominent and respected industrialist, educationist and philanthropist of Pakistan. He is a descendant of the Faqir Brothers who were both ministers of Maharaja Ranjit Singh, the ruler of Punjab (1799-1839). Babar Ali, his wife and their children and grandchildren conversed with us in Urdu. When they visited Hyderabad some years later, I tried and succeeded only partially in breaking the formality of the language of discourse. That practice still persists amongst Punjabis on both sides of the border.

Talking of the linguistic kaleidoscope of the Punjab, I am reminded of the census survey of 1951. There was a campaign amongst Hindus to register their mother tongue as Hindi while the Sikhs correctly registered Punjabi. The motive was to show Hindi as the dominant language of the state. The amusing aspect of the whole charade was that the entire campaign on both sides was conducted through Urdu papers because that was the language most adults read and wrote.

To return to the main story, I used to top my exams in all subjects except maths in which I just managed to pass. That weakness has continued right up to my third generation. I was very fond of reading and my father encouraged me by buying me a lot of books. I came to own so many books that while still at school, I started a private library in my house. Some students wanted to start a cricket team in the school. The principal of the school agreed but said that he could not trust anyone of them to keep the playing material in safe custody. Thereupon the students approached me and persuaded me to become the non-playing captain of the team.

My parents had several children of which four sons and two daughters survived. Ours was a happy family and my parents gave us an excellent education at home. My father taught us English, Mathematics, Urdu and some Persian. He made us practise good handwriting and even some calligraphy. He was a very good and patient tutor for all his children and seven grandchildren. My mother had done matriculation in English and graduation in Hindi. She tutored us in Hindi and rudimentary Sanskrit.

All of us were given elementary tuition in classical Indian music. My two brothers who had good 'voice' learnt the harmonium and vocal music. My sisters were coached in *sitar*. Since it was decided that I did not have the 'voice', I was put through a course in *tabla*. At that time tabla was treated merely as an accompanying instrument. I had therefore to depend upon one of my siblings to oblige me to enable me to show off my proficiency. It was much later that Zakir Hussain gave it the status of an independent instrument.

My parents had adopted an orphan boy of a distant relative from my father's village before having any child of their own. Named Inder Sain, he grew into a very accomplished photographer and set up his studio in the upmarket McLeod Road of Lahore. When he started earning enough money, he invited our parents from Shimla to come and select a car for him. By the time they arrived, he had gone into a delirium and died mumbling about the look of the car he fancied. We were left with many albums of photographs taken by him. However, a handful of photographs survived the Partition.

Vimla was the eldest child, about twelve years senior to me. She was a beautiful girl and had just finished her matriculation, when a handsome, young, unemployed Sikh graduate engineer saw her at the Mall in Shimla and asked for her hand in marriage. He rose to be chief engineer of irrigation of the Punjab. She was very artistic and used to recite folk songs of Punjab and Haryana. She introduced me to Amrita Pritam's immortal poem on Warris Shah. If she had lived, she would certainly have written books. She died childless while undergoing surgery shortly after the Partition.

My eldest brother, Surendra, also known as Tikka Saab by family, was seven years my senior. He was considerably indulged by our parents. He became an automobile engineer and opened his own workshop in Lahore. After the Partition, he worked in various companies and retired from the Escorts Company in Faridabad. After both his sons migrated to America, he and his wife also followed suit. His wife died a few years before him. We often talked over the phone. He missed India but could not travel so far due to health issues. He passed away in 2015 aged ninety-one.

About five years younger than him was my sister, Nirmala, nicknamed Nimmi. She, my younger brother, Virendra (Vijay), and I formed an intimate trio. She got engaged to Kartar Singh, a cousin of Vimla's husband while we were still in Lahore. He was a brilliant chemical technologist. Nimmi was married shortly after the Partition when all of us were in straitened circumstances. After considerable hardship, he was able to realize his ambition to establish a rubber factory in Faridabad.

Vijay and I remained close till his migration to America in 1990. We shared our secrets, ambitions and dreams.

He was the most intelligent and generally the most difficult amongst all my siblings. A man of many talents, both intellectual and artistic, he was a good singer, played the harmonium and the harmonica and learnt Kathak dance, but gave it up when some of us started teasing him for being effeminate. He was quite the dandy and enjoyed designing his own clothes from an early age.

He was at home both in science and the arts and I always sought his help to learn about the mystery of modern gadgetry.

We frequently played chess in which game I could never beat him.

*

Our family had a good sense of verbal humour. Only I took it into print at an early age.

We read about the caste system in our history books but never realized it applied to us too. Once a school teacher of mine asked me which caste I belonged to. I did not know and so I asked my father. He told me not to bother about it. My younger brother and I felt that our parents and close relations felt a little cagey about the question. In a low confidential tone, one of my aunts told us that we belonged to the low sub-caste of 'goldsmiths'. The *baradari* – the clan of 'goldsmiths' as a whole – tried to label themselves as 'Rajputs' so as to fall under the category of *Kshatriyas* – the second among the four Hindu castes. With that in view, all the boys had 'Singh' as the suffix to their names. We made fun of the reason for the apparent inferiority complex on that count. Just to tease our elders, Vijay used to deliberately add 'goldsmith' after his name whenever he was introduced to someone. When we later saw how people tried to get into a backward class to get the benefit of reservation, we wondered how much we had lost by staying away from this classification.

Muslims were in majority of 53.2 per cent in the Punjab according to the census of 1941. However, Hindus and Sikhs enjoyed a superior economic and social status. There was a general communal harmony amongst various communities.

Both my grandfathers died around the age of sixty. My maternal grandfather died in 1939 after a prolonged illness. My paternal grandfather followed suit the next year. He came home, lay down and passed away – apparently of cardiac arrest, something we knew little about in those days. It was attributed to his 'saintliness'. There were lengthy ceremonies on their death. I was six years old at that time.

I remember someone brought a planchette soon after my maternal grandfather's demise and, during the spells between mourning, the gathered relatives would summon my grandfather's soul to ask it where it was and how it was doing. It was very exciting to see how one could communicate with a departed soul. Later, as we grew up, someone introduced us to another, simpler version of the planchette called 'Ouija'. Small pieces of paper with letters of the English alphabet written each on a scrap of paper were placed in a rough circle. An inverted glass tumbler was placed in its centre. All the children would sit in a sort of circle. Three children would place two fingers each lightly on top of the inverted tumbler. A designated child would start by asking a dead person whether he was available. The tumbler would move from letter to letter and make a word. If it formed 'yes', we could proceed with our questions. Everyone had a suspicion that one of the children was pushing the glass. However, everyone swore that they were not playing foul. All the participants got their turn to place their fingers on the back of the tumbler, and to ask questions. We were warned that if any rude question was asked, the glass would explode into our faces. It was very popular during the summer vacation when we had a lot of time on our hands.

There was a prolonged period of mourning after the death of my paternal grandfather. Outstation relations were informed of the death through postcards which were slightly torn to signify that the card carried inauspicious news. Relatives who came from far and near used to start wailing as soon as they entered the street in which our house was located. They were met by our parents outside and then all of them cried loudly as they embraced each other. They would settle into normalcy soon after condolences were offered. For many days, professional women mourners would come from the old part of Lahore to our house. Clad in black robes they led the women of the extended bereaved family in a formal mourning drill. Forming a circle, the professional wailers would start with a rhythmic wailing tune referring to the deceased as *'sher'* (lion) if he was a young man, or *'raja'* if he was old. The women of the mourning families followed their lead in chorus. Accompanying the wailing was the rhythmic breast-beating, thigh-tapping and cheek-pinching to further dramatize the rituals of mourning. The drill started at a slow tempo but reached a crescendo after which there was a break for rest. For us children it provided great amusement especially when we noticed the pretense of some of the participants. This practice ceased in our family once we left Lahore. There, one could neither avoid professional mourners when someone died nor the *hijras*—eunuchs as they were then called—when someone was born in the family. The mourning family did not celebrate any festival for a full year. Purchase of new clothes and toys was also postponed.

Our grandmothers lived much longer. It is strange that women generally manage to outlive their husbands. I imagine it is so because they can manage widowhood better than men.

My paternal grandmother, named Gurdai, stayed mostly with us. She was looked after better in our house. She used to make incomparable *moni* rotis in Lahore. Made of equal amount of flour and ghee and a pinch of salt, they were as brittle as they were tasty. Of course that treat cost a lot and our mother allowed them only now and then.

After evening meals, all the children would snuggle into the grandmother's bed and listen to her bedtime stories and folk songs. The songs were generally about some folk tales or the misery which young girls had to suffer in their in-laws' house, particularly at the hands of mothers-in-law. They often moved us to tears, more so when we had grown up, understood the context, and saw concrete evidence at close quarters. Right until the Partition, she always used her spinning wheel humming some folk song. There was such poignant poetry in those anonymous folk songs. My mother also knew quite a few of those songs and thereafter my sister Nimmi and I attempted to sing some of those half-remembered songs whenever we met. With Nimmi's death in 2012 that too ended. Now no one even knows about those folk songs. I wish I had recorded them during Nimmi's lifetime.

*

For my high school I was enrolled in D.A.V. High School Lahore. The prevalent system of education was such that in matriculation we only repeated in English what we had learnt earlier in the eighth class in Urdu. It was therefore a waste of two years but nobody gave any thought to that practice.

My school was rated highly for its standard of academic staff and studies. It produced the largest number of winners of scholarship in the university. Because of that most Hindu boys went to that school while most Muslim boys went to the rival Islamia High School.

Every class in the school had several sections graded according to the marks obtained by students. Thus 'A' section consisted of the brightest students. I was admitted in that section of class IX. Students of that section were treated as studs in a farm and were given a free glass of milk each during the recess to fortify their bodies and sharpen their minds to win scholarships in the university examination. Screening was done in every quarterly examination. Those who slipped in their performance were shunted down to a lower section and better performers from lower sections were brought in to that special section.

In my third quarterly test, I scored low in science which comprised physics and chemistry. It was not easy to accept the disgrace of expulsion from the elite 'A' section. I told my father that I found it impossible to memorize the number of elements in chemistry which I think numbered ninety-three at that time. He allowed me to change my grouping of subjects. I opted for the other combination which comprised Urdu and drawing. To save me from embarrassment in the school, he pulled me out and got me enrolled in the Government High School in Baghban Pura, a suburb of Lahore. The school had a majority of Muslim students.

I was back to my old form in the new school and stood first in all the subjects. My English teacher created a scandal by awarding me 102 marks out of 100. He defended it by saying that not only were my answers all correct, but also my handwriting and originality was outstanding. The headmaster called for my answer sheets and after scrutiny, upheld the decision of the teacher. My Urdu maulvi taunted my Muslim classmates, asking them what sort of Muslims they were if a Hindu boy could beat them in Urdu!

My desk-mate was a handsome boy named Munir Akhtar. He was easily the best student amongst all the Muslim boys. We were good friends but our juvenile political affiliation was sharply opposed. I was a worshipper of Nehru whereas he adored Jinnah. Whenever we were free, we used to bicker about our respective idols. I believed that either he would become a civil servant or a politician. During my visit to Pakistan in 2005 mentioned earlier, I made some attempt to have him traced but did not succeed.

Heightened political activity strained the normal communal harmony in the Punjab. Many Muslim leaders belonged to the Congress party and opposed Jinnah and the Muslim League. No one imagined at that time that it was so easy to destroy the edifice built by centuries of co-existence between Hindus and Muslims.

My father was transferred to Rawalpindi in late 1946 and we moved further west when I was in class X and my university exams were about six months away.

***

Bloody Independence

India became independent on 15 August 1947. Independence in the north, particularly in the Punjab and Bengal, had two facets – one of freedom and the other of partition of the country. It was independence for those who were not disturbed from their homes and hearths. It was partition for an estimated twenty million people who were uprooted from their moorings and became penniless refugees. Undergoing an unforgettable trauma, they set a record of the biggest human migration in history. Bloody riots preceded and followed India's independence in which over one million people were estimated to have been killed. Countless women were raped. Thousands were abducted. No Punjabi household was ever the same again.

Before narrating my experience of the Partition, let me give you a brief historical background.

*

The struggle for freedom from the British rule which had been going on for a long time picked up during and after the Second World War (1939-1945), and accelerated after that. While the Indian National Congress party wanted freedom of the country as a whole, the Muslim League party declared that Muslims could not live in a country with a Hindu majority. It passed a resolution in 1940 demanding the creation of a new country to be called Pakistan comprising those provinces of India which had a Muslim majority.

Britain had lost about half a million young men and women in the war. Physically and financially it had been bled dry by the war. As a result, it ceased to be a world power. In the elections held in 1945, the Labour Party was voted to power.

While various plans for the independence of India were under discussion, on 16 August 1946 the Muslim League launched Direct Action to force its demand for Pakistan. That meant resort to violence to achieve Pakistan. It was launched in Kolkata because Bengal had a Muslim League government. That unleashed what has been called the Great Calcutta Killings. It was an unabashed state-patronized campaign for the massacre of non-Muslims, and loot and arson of their property. The scale of rioting was so severe in Noakhali that Mahatma Gandhi proceeded to the place to bring about peace.

As a reaction to the Bengal riots, there were anti-Muslim riots in Bihar and UP. Though the Punjab was a Muslim majority province, it did not have a Muslim League government. The ruling coalition was the Unionist Party. It was a secular party representing the interests of the Punjab's large feudal classes and gentry in coalition with the Congress and the Akali Dal (Sikh).

The Muslim League started an agitation in Lahore on 4 March 1947. Processions of students and women marched through the streets shouting provocative and aggressive slogans like '*Lad ke leinge Pakistan, Jaise liya tha Hindustan*' (We will get Pakistan by force just as we had once taken Hindustan). Fiery speeches were delivered by leaders at numerous places. As a result of that, rioting and arson soon broke out and spread all over the province.

The massacre of Hindus and Sikhs fleeing from the Muslim majority areas to Amritsar in trains started on 6 March 1947. It was on the basis of such brutal incidents that on 2 April 1947 Hindus and Sikhs demanded the partition of the Punjab province as against the Muslim League's demand for the whole of the Punjab.

Considering the overall situation, the new Labour government of Britain announced on 20 February 1947 that India would be granted freedom by June 1948. Lord Louis Mountbatten was appointed the new viceroy of India on 21 February 1947 to continue the negotiations with Indian leaders to that end.

After prolonged and tortuous discussions, Mountbatten secured their agreement to his plan and announced it on 3 June 1947. Based on this plan, the British Parliament passed the Indian Independence Act on 18 July 1947. The Act created two new dominions of India and Pakistan.

Mountbatten advanced the date of the grant of independence to India from June 1948 to 15 August 1947. He believed that such compression of timeline would help overcome the prevalent anarchy.

A British jurist, Cyril Radcliffe, was appointed chairman of the Boundary Commission to partition the Punjab and Bengal. He arrived in India on 8 July 1947 and had only five weeks to complete his job. He was assisted by four judges – two Muslims, one Hindu and one Sikh. He did not attend any hearings by the commission. Transcripts of the hearings were provided to him every day. Radcliffe submitted his Award to Mountbatten on 13 August 1947. The latter released it on 16 August 1947 – a day after India's independence and two days after the creation of Pakistan. It was indeed strange that two countries were created without demarcating their boundaries. The uncertainty and the unexpected demarcation of borders gave rise to heightened anger and ferocity of rioting.

Thus, there were two intense spells of rioting and arson. From 4 March 1947 to the close of the month and, after a lull, from 16 August to November 1947 and beyond, till the religious 'cleansing' was complete.

All this I know now. At that time, as a teenager I knew only what I heard from my father and other adults around. Some of those things happened to people we had known. Some of the stories were first-person accounts from the wretched survivors.

*

Starting with the epic war of *Mahabharata*, the Punjab seems to have been the divinely designated battleground of India for ages. The land of five rivers has seldom had two generations without witnessing any conflict. It was about to create a record of sorts of a century of comparative peace since its annexation by the British in 1849, when the unprecedented bloodbath of the partition of the province ensued in 1947.

This recurrent spectre of uncertainty about the future has given rise to the dominant trait in the average Punjabi's character which emphasizes living in the present discounting the prospect of the future. The following saying, originating during the multiple raids of Ahmad Shah Abdali on India in the eighteenth century, is still current in the Punjab:

Khada pita lahe da
Baki Ahmed Shahe da
(To eat and drink is all we know
For, the rest to Ahmed Shah doth go)[1]

*

[1] Khushwant Singh's translation

During the two spells of rioting we were in Rawalpindi. It is now the twin city of Islamabad, the new capital of Pakistan founded in 1967.

After Lahore and Amritsar, Rawalpindi was the third largest city of the Punjab. It had a population of about 8,00,000, about eighty per cent of which was Muslim. In the rural areas of the district the population of Muslims was even higher. A good number of them were ex-army personnel who owned weapons and were proficient in their use. Rawalpindi was virtually the gateway to the lawless tribal areas of the North West Frontier Province with its capital Peshawar 144 kilometres from Rawalpindi. The tribals were fiercely independent and enjoyed autonomy under the British Raj and have a special status now in Pakistan.

Many Sikhs had come to inhabit this region after Maharaja Ranjit Singh's annexation of Peshawar from Afghanistan in 1819. They were mostly engaged in business, commerce and moneylending and owned large properties. They came to be referred to as Bhapé. These Sikhs did not have the martial spirit generally associated with the Sikhs. The Hindus were generally in services and in business.

At the beginning of March was the first bout of riots and several Hindus and Sikhs were killed in Muslim majority localities of the city and its outskirts. The English daily *The Tribune* was the sole source of news and was published from Lahore; due to rioting, its publication and distribution had become irregular. All India Radio reported major incidents and rumours had a field day – and they were always scary.

The frequency and ferocity of rioting increased with each passing day. Frequent curfew was imposed on various localities and passes were issued generally only to government officials and other needy persons.

I wrote my matriculation exams in March 1947. The city was under curfew and students going to examination centres were given special passes. We had hardly started waiting for results when it was announced that the answer papers from a number of centres had been burnt due to arson. So, another examination was held in June. Once again the answer sheets were burnt and so the results could not be declared. By that time the situation had deteriorated so much that there was no question of holding another examination.

We were staying in Krishan Nagar, a Hindu locality separated from the Muslim-dominated locality by a small seasonal stream called Nala Lai. Tribals descended from Peshawar and the dreaded North-West Frontier and joined the locals in attacking our locality. One day, when we heard the staccato sounds of gunfire from nearby, we went up to the terrace to see where it was coming from. A bullet hit one of the neighbours on the terrace and so we rushed downstairs in panic. All able-bodied males, even as young as fourteen like me, were asked to do night patrolling in relays. We were given whatever arms were available. I was given a broken rusted sword and cautioned that I should not die like a dog. Some of the houses like ours had covered wells in their courtyards. On the basis of the harrowing accounts of rape of women from different places, womenfolk were instructed that in case of massacre of menfolk, they should jump into wells and commit suicide to 'save their honour'. Such acts of mass suicides had already been reported from outlying areas of the district.

In early July my mother was admitted in the government hospital for some surgery and she stayed on for the delivery of a baby. My youngest brother, Arendra, also known as Gogo, was born on 21 July 1947. At the hospital we saw some buses enter the hospital carrying a number of dead bodies and severely wounded persons. A group of Hindus had tried to flee to Srinagar by road. They were waylaid and attacked by rioters. I felt giddy at the sight of blood and raw wounds.

By early August, we could no longer hold out against the rioters. We therefore moved into the heart of the city in an area called Bazaar-e-Saraffan (Jeweller's Street) which was mostly inhabited by Hindus. The Sarna family distantly related to us had a jewellery shop and a house close by, and they took us in.

Cooped up in the sitting room in that house we heard Pandit Nehru's speech on the midnight of 14-15 August 1947 shivering with emotion that we had become a free nation. Outside there were no festivities. An eerie silence enveloped the deserted streets broken by occasional gunshots and rumblings of menacing slogans in the distance. From time to time someone or the other pulled the curtains aside to see the ember glow of fires on the horizon.

A fresh and more ferocious spell of rioting, loot and arson broke out when the boundaries of the two countries were announced on 16 August 1947.

Earlier all government personnel had been asked to exercise their option whether they wanted to serve in India or Pakistan. My father had opted for Pakistan believing that it would only mean a change in the governor-general. 'Now it is Mountbatten and tomorrow it will be Jinnah. The common man will not be affected,' was his simplistic reassurance to my mother and others who believed that he knew better. I learned later many other government servants had done likewise.

Akram and Aslam

His option was soon nullified by mounting riots and arson. When life became difficult even in the city, the Muslim superintendent in my father's office suggested that the families of two Hindu officers should shift to his son's house. He was a junior commissioned officer in the army and stayed in the cantonment and intended to send his wife and children to her parents' home for a few days till the situation improved. Two families and a bachelor officer gratefully accepted the offer and moved into his rather small house. There they ran a common kitchen, divided the chores and shared the expenses. Boys were given strict instructions that anyone who moved out of the house should assume Muslim names. I took on the name Akram and my younger brother Vijay became Aslam. They were easy to remember and we got used to them even at home. Thanks to my father's instruction, I could easily recite the *Kalima*.[2] I made Vijay learn it but warned him not to pee in the open. That would be a fatal exposure!

Soon it became clear that there was no prospect of any improvement in the situation. The only question was how soon we could manage to leave safely for India. An exodus started as religious frenzy took hold of the majority community and lawlessness and consequent rioting increased. Government officials, including policemen, started showing their communal bias with every passing day. Gradually, even the army was infected by the communal virus. Only the Gurkha units could be trusted to be completely impartial.

Every morning my father went to various offices to seek information about the arrangements for the evacuation of non Muslim officials and their families. The administration was grappling with the problem of ensuring a smooth flow of refugees. A vast majority from rural areas formed into village-wise caravans and started marching on foot to the safety of some nearby town.

[2] *La ilaha ill Allah Muhammadur-Rasul Allah* (There is no God but Allah, Muhammad is the Messenger of Allah)

When they found the situation no better there, they resumed the march to somehow reach across the newly drawn frontiers. Some of those caravans were miles in length. Men, women, children and cattle trudged the unchartered terrain making new paths for others to follow. Some persons carried their old parents and grandparents on their shoulders or on string-cots and charpoys. As the long, weary trek stretched endlessly, some old and infirm people fell behind and died of exhaustion and hunger. Those who were too old and sick pleaded with their children to leave them behind and carry on without them. We heard hair-raising accounts about many who were thus abandoned. While the hapless caravans crawled on, some hooligans ambushed them from adjoining fields of sugar cane crop. They looted their belongings, killed the menfolk if they resisted, and picked up women and raped them openly. Some women were also abducted. Womenfolk could not be saved. The attackers were young, armed and in a state of frenzy. The defenders were hungry, fatigued and helpless.

We stayed in the Chaklala cantonment for over a month. Every evening my father returned with the news about the murder of someone or the other we had known. We heard our parents discuss in subdued voices about money running out. They ended up reassuring each other hoping their luck would hold out. Amongst them the elders of three families discussed how to cope with the dark, uncertain future. My father had locked and sealed our house in Krishen Nagar. On the door he had pasted the address of my maternal uncle in Amritsar in case anyone wanted to contact him. One day he came with the news that our house had already been occupied by a family from across the Nala. We took in the news calmly as if it was about someone else. It did not seem to matter.

Property did not matter. Good fortune was to escape the fate of the caravan people, to get away with the family unharmed, with the honour of women intact.

Our worldly possessions now were only two steel trunks containing summer clothes and two holdalls stuffed with summer beddings and some miscellaneous items for a family of six – my parents, my elder sister, my brother Vijay, me, and the new infant, Gogo. My eldest sister, Vimla, was already married and her husband was posted in the irrigation department of the Indian part of Punjab. Tikka Saab, the brother next in line, was already in India.

*

On 17 October 1947 my father returned with the tidings that a special train for government servants would be leaving for Amritsar the next day. We packed our meagre belongings in no time. We had expected reserved seats in the train. However, when we reached the Chaklala railway station we saw a sea of surging humanity with all sorts of baggage already there. There was no question of reservation; it was free for all. An unusually long train could be seen at some distance.

There were very few coolies and they demanded fifty rupees a piece to carry the baggage. My father, Vijay and I carried the trunks. My sister and mother managed to drag the bedrolls till I was able to come back to carry one. We made for the nearest compartment. The first batch of occupants tried in vain to block entry to newcomers saying there was no accommodation. Those outside first begged and then became abusive and aggressive. The occupants had to relent more out of fear than sympathy. More families arrived by the minute. They did not ask, did not care and shoved their baggage through the door which had been half-barred by the pressure of baggage of the occupants. 'There is no space,' someone shouted from inside. 'Never mind, we will go and sit on the roof. Just let our bags in.' Soon there were more people on the roof of the train than inside. A large number of men clung to the doors and windows of compartments.

Our compartment carried a notice in English and Urdu: 'To seat 17 persons only.' I counted thirty men, women and children.

Soon the small compartment became a mound of trunks, bedrolls and all sorts of packets, big and small. Children clambered up the heaps of baggage and made a sport of rolling down, going up, and rolling down repeatedly.

We were relieved to notice that platoons of Gurkha soldiers mounted guard in front of the engine, in the middle of the train, and behind the last compartment of the train. They were protected by sandbags and armed with machine guns.

Having settled down in the safety of the compartment, all of us heaved a sort of collective sigh of relief. Across from us a newly married young couple sat snuggled together, the woman still in her bridal finery and forearms covered with ivory and multicoloured glass bangles. An old woman sat next to the man, probably his mother. Looking at the young couple, Vijay and I exchanged mischievous, knowing glances about what they might be feeling. Armed Gurkha soldiers patrolled the length of the train on both sides a number of times before they gave the all-clear. Then we heard the guard's whistle. The engine hooted in response and the train started moving slowly. Soon it was dusk and the compartment was only lit dimly. Passengers began opening their packets of food – stuffed parathas and other snacks for the evening meal, some offering to share their food with others, a tradition of railway journeys in the country.

We were in the middle of our meal when we heard the sound of gunfire. The train came to a sudden halt and then began to reverse. After what seemed to be a long time, the gunfire became sporadic and then stopped. After that there was nothing to do except to try and sleep. But there was no place to even stretch our limbs. I dreamt I was sleeping on a plush bed in a palace. A jolt of the train woke me up and I found that I was lying on a heap of luggage. Such dreams came in repeated short snatches. Everyone was probably having similar dreams. It was indeed a long night. My father pulled out his pocket watch off and on and announced the time for general benefit. At long last, dawn peeped through the window shutters. Some people starting going to the toilet, the door of which was somehow kept free from any obstruction. Someone announced that we should be reaching Lahore soon. My father lifted the window shutter to check the name of the station the train was passing by. We were barely halfway to Lahore. He saw a crowd at the platform waving for the train to stop. Presumably they were refugees like us waiting to be evacuated. But the train did not stop. It was already overloaded and there was a risk that there might be an ambush. Those were not the times when people were bothered much about others.

About an hour later the train stopped again. Again there was the sound of exchange of fire. Someone climbed down from the roof and said that a burning tree had been laid across the rails and a crowd, shouting slogans and firing shots, had surrounded the front of the train not knowing that the train had a Gurkha escort. Instinctively, my mother stopped distributing whatever was left of the stock of our parathas. She whispered to us that we had to make do till we reached Lahore. 'There we can buy something more to eat,' she offered by way of reassurance. We understood.

Ah! Lahore

But the whole day passed and there was no sign of Lahore. The train stopped twice more for extended periods. The sound of sloganeering mobs and the sight of distant arson accompanied by exchange of fire between the rioters and Gurkhas made us down the window shutters, keep quiet and hope for the best. For the time being hunger and thirst were kept at bay.

The train picked up speed and Vijay, still 'Aslam', started reciting *chal chal fata fut, chal chal fata fut* – a children's rhyme mimicking the sound produced by wheels of an express train. That lifted the tension in the compartment.

In the evening the train stopped again and the same story was repeated. Each time a palpable fear glued together everybody in the compartment and imposed a curfew of silence. What kept our hope up was the knowledge that the Gurkhas were defending us.

There was another problem now. We were hungry but by evening there was nothing left to eat. All our provisions had been exhausted. We – my sister Nimmi, Vijay and I – understood, but the infant Gogo did not. The milk powder tin still had enough powder, but there was no water to make milk. My mother tried to feed him a small spoon of milk powder. Gogo opened his small mouth eagerly but in an instant spat it out. Nimmi tried to cajole him in a maternal sort of way into accepting the powder: 'Gogo, there is nothing else. Take it baby.' Instead, Gogo fumbled for mother's breast. My mother obliged him but not finding any milk there, he bit her nipple. She howled in pain and withdrawing her breast uttered the customary Punjabi curse for boys: *Daffa ho* – get lost. Incidentally, the rebukes for girls were – and I suppose, continue to be – much more severe: *Sir sadhi* and *Mar jaani* – both wishing death upon them, or worse still, *Khasmaa khaani* – eater of husband or widowhood! A knowing mother cursing her offspring of her own sex!

Gogo resumed his crying. Overtaken by sudden remorse, my mother caught him in tight embrace. That quietened him and a feeling of peace returned to the whole compartment.

One can do without food much longer than without water. The panic resulting from the knowledge that there was no water accentuated our thirst. Our lips were parched as happens during illness or by prolonged exposure to the sun. Were we going to die that way? We would soon be reaching Lahore, my father consoled us. We could get some water there. Those days the railways supplied free drinking water to passengers. One man with a metal pitcher of water and a long-handled dispensing ladle would pass by every compartment announcing 'Hindu *paani*, Hindu *paani*'. All Hindu passengers would project their receptacles through the window and get them filled up with water. He was followed by another water carrier announcing 'Muslim *paani*, Muslim *paani*' and Muslim passengers followed the earlier drill. Nobody gave any thought to the fact that water came from the same overhead tank at the station. Only the carriers were Hindu or Muslim!

Looking at my mother, Vijay said playfully, 'This is Pakistan. You won't get Hindu paani now.'

Suddenly, someone shouted 'Lahore!' We lifted the shutters of the windows. It was Lahore station indeed, but instead of slowing down, the train sped faster. The platform was barricaded on both sides with barbed wire presumably to protect the passing refugee trains from rioters. My mother remarked morosely that there had never ever been a time when a train would pass through Lahore station without halting.

Having left Lahore behind in unbecoming hurry, the train came to an unexpected halt near a small flag station called Mughal Pura. By then it was dark again. The children started crying for water. Unable to bear the sight, my father stole out of the compartment with a small bucket and returned after a while with water from a pond close to the railway track. He had taken a serious risk in doing that since both the Gurkha guards or the rioters could have assaulted him, or killed him. The water smelt strongly of DDT. He asked us to just take a sip each, no more. But we were dying of thirst and so everybody drank much more than a sip. The mild dose of lethal liquid hit our empty stomachs. Soon we were holding our aching bellies and throwing up. The stink of vomit filled the compartment. It looked as if the children were all dying. My father looked on helplessly. Had he poisoned his children!

A young man descended from the roof of our compartment and rushed in pushing the door to announce that three persons from the roof of the adjoining compartment had been killed by firing. He begged to be allowed to stay in the compartment. No one said anything. He was already there. The train stayed there for the night deepening the suspense and fear amongst the passengers.

There was nothing to eat or drink while a whole night of apprehension lay ahead. We held our stomachs, moaned with spasmodic contortions and tried to puke. But nothing came out of empty bellies.

The train jerked two or three times raising our hopes about the resumption of our journey, but it did not start.

Finally morning light came in through the shutters. The train started moving again, stopped once more briefly and then started moving forward slowly. Vijay started reciting a Punjabi doggerel about a slow train: *'Chal chalnaa hi keh...'* (No hurry, we are moving...)

The train stopped one more time for no apparent reason. There seemed to be no attack or any exchange of firing. After a while it started and picked up speed.

Just around noon suddenly someone in the compartment shouted 'Hindustan'. We quickly opened the window shutters and saw people waving to us in friendly gestures from their fields on both sides. Farmers, men, women and children, standing in the midst of their harvest of sugar cane crop were waving Indian pennants. The train, feeling at home after a long journey, slowed down and an exchange of loud and raucous slogans rent the air. *'Hindustan Zindabad,' 'Mahatma Gandhi ki Jai'* and *'Bharat Mata ki Jai.'* A current ran through the gloomy compartment – indeed the whole train – and puking children, miraculously revived. We felt transported magically onto the roads and streets of Lahore of 1946 when we used to join medley processions shouting the selfsame slogans that we were now hearing from the peasants in the sugar cane fields passing by our train, frame by frame.

The entire train – the compartments and their roofs – reverberated with the sound of answering slogans. In an instant the train became a procession moving slowly, smoothly to the rhythm of slogans.

The engine hooted hoarsely announcing its arrival at freedom's gate.

Just as suddenly and miraculously had we recovered from our sickness that my father fell seriously ill. He could hardly speak, or even get up.

On the noon of 21 October 1947 our train, exhausted from the long journey carrying a human cargo many times its normal load, steamed into the Amritsar railway station. Yes, two dates – 18 and 21 October are singed in my memory. So is the bilingual notice stencilled on the wall of the compartment: 'To seat 17 persons only.' That compartment was our concentration camp for two nights and three days. We had suffered five armed attacks on the way. And survived! How lucky!

Amritsar is only fifty kilometres from Lahore. How many times had we travelled between the two cities by train or bus! Radcliffe had knifed a line close to Amritsar to mark the border between the two new countries.

Amritsar was the second biggest city of the Punjab. It was also one of the worst riot-affected districts in Punjab. As early as 13 August 1947, the governor of the Punjab, Sir Evan Jenkins, reported in his daily telegrams to the viceroy, Lord Mountbatten, that 'Lahore urban area and Amritsar district are out of control.'[3]

Young men clinging to door handles and window bars of the train released their weary grips, slid down to the platform and started trotting along with the slowing train. Those perched on the roof of the train started jumping down even before the train came to a halt.

Immediately, a group of young, earnest volunteers from the platform came peering into every compartment asking if there were any dead bodies inside. There were none in our compartment.

As we came out of the train, we noticed a makeshift cremation ground to our left at some distance from the platform. Some bodies were burning there. Nine bodies were recovered from our train. They were taken to the cremation site, their wailing and sobbing families following them. We were led to the right side where we drank water from the taps nearby. After that we were asked to sit down

[3] Ajit Bhattacharjea, *Countdown to Partition – the Final Days* (India: HarperCollins, 1997), p. 101

in multiple parallel rows. A relay of men and women distributed leaf-plates and served us dal and dry rotis similar to the free *langar* in Sikh gurdwaras.

We laid our father on a makeshift bed made by joining two trunks and a bedroll since he could not sit. He waived away all offers of any food or water.

The sight of burning bodies and the acrid smell of new bodies recovered from the train and laid out in a line to await their turn for cremation did not affect the appetizing smell of the food being served to us. We lapped up the dal and rotis like famished beggars.

October was the herald of winter in the Punjab. The festival of Dussehra generally falls in late October or early November. Customarily, the day also signalled the harvesting of sugar cane crop. After burning the giant effigy of the demon king Ravana in the *maidan*, sugar cane sticks were brought home and distributed to all members of the family. Everybody chewed sugar cane pieces. But that October no one had any idea about Dussehra or Diwali – the festival of lights which followed Dussehra after a fortnight. The Punjab was bleeding in an orgy of massacre. Those who escaped were in deep mourning for their loved ones who had been killed or whose whereabouts were not known yet.

In the mild cool of the approaching winter, the glow of warmth from the tongues of flames consuming the corpses was soothing.

A loudspeaker blared out directions to the newly arrived persons about where to go for inquiries and assistance. As they finished their meals, people got up and made for different directions. Most of them proceeded towards the waiting lorries meant to take them to camps set up by the government for refugees from Pakistan.

My mother's elder brother, Vidya Sagar, was professor of zoology in the Khalsa College at Amritsar. He was also a popular poet in Punjabi with a tremendous sense of humour. We had always enjoyed our visits to his house. He and my father were great buddies.

The All India Radio broadcast continuously announcing the arrival of refugee trains and their origin as also the names of families in India asking about their near and dear ones from amongst the refugees.

After finishing our meals, we hired a *tonga*, loaded our baggage onto it, and reached my uncle's house. We received a very warm welcome from the family. The elders embraced each other. Women sobbed. My father was examined by a physician and given a course of medication.

We spent a fortnight there during which period my father made a substantial recovery. In one of the radio announcements, government employees coming from Pakistan were asked to report to their respective departments which had been set up in Jalandhar. One of my father's cousins was a doctor in the jail there. He had been brought up, educated and married off by my parents and should have been beholden to them. But he gave us a very cold reception.

***

A Tumbler and a Book

In Jalandhar we were reunited with my elder sister and brother who had given us up for dead.

We did not have to suffer the frosty countenance of my father's cousin and his wife for long. My father got his posting orders to Garh Shankar, a subdivision of the district of Hoshiarpur, about thirty km away, and so we moved there. We were allotted a house from the pool of the evacuee houses. By then winter had set in. We were entirely unequipped for it. The government distributed one quilt or blanket for each member of the refugee families. In addition, one khaki woollen pullover and one pair of trousers for each family was also given from the army disposal. That is how we managed to live through our first winter in free India. Between my father and I whoever went out would use them. The rest would stay at home keeping themselves warm by the side of the hearth.

One day it was announced that the refugee families could collect the much-needed household effects from the houses left behind by Muslim evacuees. The *tahsildar* set up his office outside a large building and one member from each refugee family assembled there. I represented my family and was asked to pick up utensils and other articles of daily use. I had brought a bedsheet with me and with that I entered the Ali Baba's cave of treasures of household goods lying in scattered heaps before me. I picked up such items as I imagined would be crucially needed for the new house. After I had bundled my pick in the sheet, my eyes fell upon a white metal tumbler on which the following Urdu couplet was inscribed:

Aab-e-angoor ne to aag lagaa di Saaqi
Baraf pilaa ke kalejaa meraa thandaa kar de.
(Wine has set my innards afire, O' Saki,
Give me some iced water to soothe them)

From my early years I had been very fond of Urdu and had acquired a better than average degree of competence in the language. I liked the couplet and picked up the tumbler as a gift for myself.

Then, just as I was leaving, I noticed a copy of the Quran lying in a corner. My father's profusely annotated copy of the Quran had been left behind in Rawalpindi. So I picked it up as a gift for him.

At home everybody laughed at my choice of the tumbler. It had obviously belonged to a tippler. My father's face brightened up like a child upon receiving his gift. It was the first book in our new house.

Noticing the copy of the Quran, my eldest sister asked me somewhat agitatedly, 'Why have you brought the book that brought so much ruin upon us?' My father admonished her gently and said that it was because of that book that we were all alive. 'Do not forget that we were given asylum by one of the followers of this book.'

That copy of the Quran is still with me.

*

I had appeared twice already for my matriculation examination in Rawalpindi without getting any result. There were innumerable such cases and the government did not have the wherewithal to conduct examinations afresh. It therefore decided that two months of social service in a refugee camp would entitle candidates to the certificate/degree for which they said they had appeared in Pakistan. It was on the basis of trust and good faith and of course it was abused in many cases. Many persons became graduates and even post-graduates on the basis of false declarations. Many also secured government jobs on the basis of such degrees. For many years after independence, candidates were asked in interviews whether they had a proper or a 'social service' degree!

I got admission in the D.A.V. College at Jalandhar and moved into the hostel. The rush for admission was so great that three students were packed into each room meant for one student. One of the senior students became over friendly with me and used to get into my bed and try to fondle me. I did not know how to shake him off or to complain against him. Luckily for me, when the Rashtriya Swayamsevak Sangh was banned after Mahatma Gandhi's assassination on 30 January 1948, he was arrested along with some other students. Meanwhile I joined up with the Nanda brothers in a new room. My tormentor returned after three months, a self-pitying martyr with a beard, but I was able to keep my distance from him. Subsequently, when some of us shifted to a new house, another senior made similar advances to me. He later became a political leader and was elected to the state legislative assembly.

The two-year intermediate course was compressed into one year to make up for lost time. By that time the government had given soft loans to refugees for buying household items and winter clothing. In the winter of 1949 our mother bought a piece of a coarse woollen cloth called '*Patti*'. In poorly stitched and ill-fitting Patti jackets, Vijay and I felt like princes.

From my hostel room I could see a large tented colony of refugees across the railway track. It was one of the biggest refugee camps in the province. Freedom made destitute of thousands of well-off people. It also imparted to them firm resolve to build a new life for themselves. Human beings are at their fighting best when they are in their worst circumstances. Young men and women of my generation had fire in their bellies.

*

For my graduation, I went to the University College Hoshiarpur to which place my father had been transferred. I stood first in the university in my BA (Honours) and won a medal and a scholarship of twenty-five rupees a month. To that was added a special scholarship of equal amount from the discretionary fund of the vice chancellor. By then I had started writing for *The Tribune*, then the only English daily in the Punjab. From my articles I started getting an average income of twenty rupees per month. Later, in a college competition, I was selected for a debate on All India Radio which had a station at Jalandhar, about thirty km from Hoshiarpur. That started me on my life-long association with All India Radio. I began earning fifteen rupees for every programme. My father had retired by then and my scattered earnings thus made a crucial contribution to the family income. It was ironic that while my programmes were broadcast quite often, we did not yet possess a radio set. One day I came home and saw a new radio set in our sitting room. 'To listen to you,' said my mother proudly. Thereafter, we did not have to go to the neighbours to listen to my programmes.

I was a shy student. But when I witnessed the first debate held in the college, I felt an irresistible urge to participate in it. The opportunity was soon provided by the annual declamation contest. I enrolled for that and practised my speech dozens of time for a fortnight. I rehearsed in the bathroom, before the mirror, before retiring to bed, first thing after getting up and whenever and wherever possible. The result was that I got the first prize beating a veteran debater who was three years my senior. That helped me come out of the shell of shyness and I started participating in college and inter-collegiate and inter-university debates. I also began taking active part in extra-curricular activities. On the basis of a competition I was selected editor of the college magazine both for the English and Urdu editions. I was also elected secretary of the students' union.

We stayed in a house close to the college and so I could walk to the college. I had only one pair of trousers and one woollen pullover which my grandmother had knitted for me. I had outgrown the Patti jacket and the pullover was not adequate to ward off the biting cold of December. One day a rich college mate of mine clad in a tweed jacket said he had taken a fancy to my pullover and wanted to exchange his jacket with my pullover. It was apparent that it was not a fair exchange and I declined the offer. He felt slighted at my refusal for the barter. Some other friend interceded and the swap deal was sealed. To this day I have always felt that he did that only to help me.

Some of the adulation I received from the students and pats from the faculty went to my head and I lost elections for the presidency of the union next year. Also I fell in love with a classmate of mine. As a result, I could not continue my earlier trail and got only a second division in my MA.

That chastened me. My experience during the elections for the students' union was so disgusting that I decided never again to take part in any electoral politics at any level. I derive vicarious satisfaction watching the contestants in this grisly game from my ivory tower.

THE HADALI COUSINS

Shimla was made the summer capital of British India in 1864. It was also the headquarters of the British Indian army. The construction of a railway line from Kalka to Shimla was taken up in 1898 and completed in 1903. It was considered a marvel of engineering and in 2008 it was nominated as a UNESCO heritage site.

The contractors for the construction were two Sikh cousins, Chanchal Singh and Sujan Singh, hailing from Hadali, a village in the Khushab district of Punjab, now in Pakistan. According to the family lore, sackfuls of money made in the project by the cousins were sent to Kalka railway station by a continuous relay of mules. From there they were transported by train to Delhi where the cousins stayed.

The cousins divided the earnings between them. Chanchal Singh went back to his village and bought huge tracts of land in the fertile stretch bounded by the rivers Chenab and Jhelum. He started growing cotton and also established eight cotton ginning mills exporting bales of cotton to Lancashire. He thus became a pioneering farmer and industrialist in the province. The younger cousin, Sujan Singh, settled down in Delhi and later became one of the contractors for building Lutyens' Delhi. He was the first private realtor and developer in India and built extensive properties including many in Connaught Place and an estate called Sujan Singh Park in New Delhi. For his own residence he built a mansion on what is now called 1-A Janpath. It is now on lease to the Hungarian Cultural Centre.

His elder son, Sobha Singh, joined his father in building New Delhi. He was knighted by the British. One of Sir Sobha Singh's sons was the renowned Khushwant Singh who, like other members of the family, was given a flat in Sujan Singh Park. I met Sir Sobha Singh one winter evening in 1963. I recall him standing tall and erect with his back to the fireplace with a glass of Scotch in his hand. He asked me casually, 'How is Chandulal faring?' 'Chandulal, who?,' I asked. He explained, '*Oe*, Trivedi.'

He was referring to the then governor of Andhra Pradesh. 'A good bridge player,' he remarked. I was impressed.

Chanchal Singh prospered as a country squire and industrialist. He sired six sons and two daughters. His elder son Khazan Singh brought his beautiful bride Kulwant Kaur home in a car from the Bhalwal railway station to the family mansion on a short road covered all the way with a carpet of cotton ginned in one of the family factories.

Communal riots erupting in March 1947 spread out to places like Bhalwal and Malakwal also. The prestige of the family and its clout with the bureaucracy, reinforced by about 200 migrant labourers from Bihar working in their factories and farms, were enough to provide adequate defense against rioters. However, organized attacks became common after 16 August 1947. Khazan Singh, thirty-seven, and his wife, a year younger, had four daughters and two sons. The eldest, a daughter, was eighteen and the youngest, was a boy about three years old. All of them were neatly spaced at an interval of about two years between each child. Very good family planning indeed!

One day a unit of the Baloch Regiment of the army came and evacuated all non-Muslims from the town and gathered them in a camp in an open field to organize their departure to India. The late Chanchal Singh's family, the Khuranas – that is the surname used by his descendents later – was also brought out to the camp. Khazan

Singh and Sampuran Singh suggested to the regiment's commander that they could accommodate the camp in their compound and also arrange for food for them. They were thus allowed to go back to their house and take care of the refugee camp.

One of Khazan Singh's cousins was a captain in the army. He sent one of his Muslim lieutenants to pick up the family in an army lorry and bring them to safety. Sampuran Singh offered to stay back and so Khazan Singh's family boarded the army lorry. His wife and all the girls put on two sets of salwar suits each. They had *potlis* (small bags) of jewellery stitched in their salwars. They were taken to the house of the young lieutenant in Jhelum, at a distance of about eighty kilometres.

Three days later they were taken to the railway station to board a special refugee train bound for Amritsar. However, they could not get accommodation for the whole family in one compartment and Khazan Singh was not willing to have them split up. They therefore turned back disappointed. It proved providential for them. The entire train was massacred on the way to Lahore. They stayed for a few more days in trepidation as guests of the lieutenant. Some days later, the young officer secured permission to take them to Lahore by an army lorry. They were asked to hide under a tarpaulin to escape the notice of rioters and hooligans. In Lahore they were put up in the army mess to await arrangements for the last lap of the journey to cross the border to India. Caravans or trains were being organized for movement of large groups. The officer again came two days later and drove them in the lorry up to Wagha, the border post. From there they walked and reached Amritsar. Khazan Singh's wife's brother Gurdial Singh was a deputy collector married to the daughter of Sardar Bahadar Hukam Singh, a prominent landlord of Amritsar.

They were accommodated in one of his houses along with some other refugee relatives. After a few days Khazan Singh was allotted an evacuee property house. They stayed there but the girls had to suffer the humiliation of going daily to the refugee camp to collect their rations. Kulwant Kaur started selling her jewellery piece by piece to supplement the meagre government assistance to the family. Those days the old parachutes of the Royal Indian Air Force started coming into the market. The material was cheap, strong and crease-proof. Refugee women began stitching their suits with that material.

Ujjal Singh, younger brother of Sir Sobha Singh and a second cousin of Khazan Singh, became finance minister of the Indian Punjab after independence. He arranged for the allotment of an iron foundry and one big house from out of the evacuee property in Batala to Khazan Singh. The house belonged to the father of Nawaz Sharif, now prime minister of Pakistan. Incidentally, I asked Nawaz Sharif about it when I met him at Riyadh during his exile there. He said he was born in Pakistan and so did not know. Only his father could certify that, but he was sick.

Khazan Singh entered into a partnership with one of his relations. It worked for a few years and the family seemed to be on the path to financial recovery. But in 1950 the industry was hit by a slump and the partner pulled out. Khazan Singh could never recover from his losses. His eldest daughter started working to support the family. The next daughter threw a tantrum insisting that she would pursue her post-graduation. A family friend offered to sponsor her education. She was given seventy rupees a month to cover her tuition fees and hostel expenses.

That daughter, called Bindi at home, enrolled for MA in political science at the University College Hoshiarpur in 1951.

Separately, I had changed my stream from economics to political science.

Fate had been working out the plot for a long time.

The entire saga of India's struggle for independence, the partition of the country – all the rioting, arson and massacre of a million people – was for the plant of tenderness to sprout, for love to happen!

And it happened. In the fall of 1952 Bindi and I fell in love.

*

Take our two separate stories, and sprinkle them liberally with abductions, rapes and murders. Multiply that a million times and you get a glimpse of the partition of the Punjab and of the horrible facet of India's independence. Partition was Punjab's holocaust. There was immaculate planning in the way the Nazis exterminated the Jews in Germany. In contrast, our communal cleansing was carried out shabbily, crudely and with a degree of brutality matching that of the hordes of Nadir Shah and Ahmad Shah Abdali we read about in history. Why go into the past? As I write this, I see every day our Partition story replicated in West Asia. The past is always with us.

Looking back over it, I am surprised that our parents did not lose their mental balance. Imagine, all their movable and immovable property was lost in the course of a few days. They were driven out of their homes on the point of bayonet virtually in little more than the clothes in which they stood. In the worst moments of life humans are capable of drawing some comfort from some compensating features. After all, no one in the family was killed. No woman in the family was abducted or molested. What they lost in comparison to innumerable other families was nothing. 'We can cope with these losses,' observed my mother. 'Even make them up,' added my father. For us children, it was an adventure of a sort and we did not understand the magnitude of the trauma fully. As we grew up, we understood and often felt its long-term impact. But my children and grandchildren do not know anything about it. So also, the people in the south of India are not aware of the cost paid by the Punjab and Bengal for India's freedom.

We did not get freedom in a bloodless revolution as our leaders often boast. A million persons paid for it with their lives; about twelve million lost all their worldly possessions and became destitute. In India they were called *sharanathi* – refugees; in Pakistan, *muhajir*s – migrants. The Indian refugees were fully integrated into the mainstream within a generation. Pakistan's refugees were congealed into a separate political party called the Muhajir Qaumi Movement – the MQM – and they are still fighting for the acknowledgement that the real price for achieving Pakistan was paid by them.

Also – and here I speak for a smaller number of people like our family – we did not lose the secular values in which we were nurtured. Faceless mobs threw us out of our homes. A Muslim saved us by giving us refuge for one whole month. Sometimes one single person atones for the sins of the whole community. The argument that there was retributive killing on both sides between Muslims and non-Muslims does not offer any consolation. But singular cases of humanity amidst raging intolerance do. We never forgot that.

* * *

DREAMS OF GLORY

Right from early childhood I heard many relatives and visitors mention to my parents that I should be groomed for ICS – Indian Civil Service. I did not understand at that time what it meant but sensed that it must be something special. In 1948, ICS was replaced by IAS – Indian Administrative Service. To enter a competition to join it was such a lofty ambition that many young persons did not even dream of it. Yet about 1,00,000 tried their luck at it annually. As school children we would hear about the deputy commissioner (collector) being so enormously powerful that he had the 'power of life and death' over people. When I was harassed by some bullies in the school, I used to pray that one day I should become a deputy commissioner so that I could send my tormentors to the gallows.

Adolescents pass through many phases, each marked by a different vision of their future. By the time I got to my MA, my ambition had narrowed down to two careers – professorship in the likeness of Harold Laski, and IAS. After my experience of the brazen favouritism shown by two selection committees that I encountered for a lectureship, I dropped my goal of being a professor. I came to the conclusion that I could succeed only in an open and fair competition.

I was not yet twenty-one when I passed my MA in 1953 and so was not eligible to sit for the competitive exam for IAS. I devoted the time for preparation and wrote the exam from Shimla in 1954. There were about six months before the declaration of the result. I therefore applied for the job of a lecturer. One of my classmates was the elder son of the late Pratap Singh Kairon, the then chief minister of the state. He was my self-styled arch-rival and used to brag about his chances of landing the job. The government selection board obliged readily by selecting him in violation of merit.

I was also overlooked for a similar vacancy in a private college at Ferozepur. A nephew of the chairman of the college committee was selected for the job. However, since the selected person could not control his class, I was offered the job at a salary of Rs 170 per month. My maternal uncle was an executive engineer posted at Ferozepur. I stayed with the family contributing Rs 50 a month keeping about Rs 25 for my out-of-pocket expenses and the rest I sent home. For two months I defaulted in sending any remittance because I was fooled into giving the entire amount to an opium addict who enacted a tragic drama at a street corner on my way to the college.

I still had my one tweed jacket and two pairs of trousers. There was no scope of supplementing my 'wardrobe', if I may use the term for a person in my circumstances. Everything was by way of a temporary arrangement; what was permanent was hope for a turn of events soon. I taught political science for five months. One fine morning *The Tribune* carried my name amongst the fifty who had been selected for IAS. Suddenly, I became the toast of the town. Congratulatory telegrams started pouring in from all over. My students were so thrilled that they would not let me teach anymore and started organizing farewell parties for me.

*

Indian Civil Service was devised by the East India Company for managing its trade in India. Young boys sent out by the Company to India between the ages of thirteen and fifteen were recruited as 'writers'. Every director was authorized to nominate one recruit while the chairman and deputy chairman could nominate two each.

Due to high mortality amongst the employees and the expanding role they came to play with the rise in the Company's fortunes, they came to be entrusted with a variety of jobs, including that of soldiers, judges and even chaplains.

In 1772 Warren Hastings, the governor-general of the East India Company, split the territory under the Company into units called 'districts'. Each district was under the charge of a British officer called 'collector'.

The collector became the lynchpin of the administrative structure of the Company. In course of time, the ICS officers came to be known for their efficiency, versatility and integrity. Satyendranath Tagore, elder brother of the famous poet Rabindranath Tagore, was the first Indian to make it to the ICS in 1864.

ICS officers came to enjoy such power, prestige and emoluments that the service acquired the sobriquet of 'heaven-born' service. In 1922, British Prime Minister Lloyd George called ICS the 'Steel Frame' of the Indian constitutional structure.

The mystique of the ICS and the popular fascination with it was such that it was the dream of the brightest and the best Indians to enter it. Aurobindo Ghosh passed the examination, but was disqualified in the riding test presumably because of some secret adverse reports about him. Netaji Subhash Chandra Bose also qualified in 1920, but resigned soon afterwards. Dr Rajendra Prasad wanted to go to England to compete for the service. However, his orthodox relatives blocked his journey to England. He later became the first president of India.

Many members of the ICS took keen interest in extra-curricular fields. Their work in compiling grammars of various languages, translation of Indian classics, writing on Indian history, study of anthropology, codification of Indian laws, devising social welfare measures and introducing reforms in the social sector is outstanding. There is hardly any sphere of intellectual and literary activity which does not bear their impress.

The district gazetteers compiled by the members of the service still remain the best 'Google' on districts.

It was this aspect of the work of ICS officers that impelled the famous Communist leader R. Palme Dutt (1896-1974) to remark that 'the ICS as a body had made the largest single contribution of knowledge about India'.[4]

I dreamt of belonging to the special category of such administrator-scholars.

*

I reported for training in Delhi on 25 May 1955.

Our batch consisted of fifty IAS and IFS (Indian Foreign Service) recruits. Subsequently seven more joined later at various stages. Ten of them were members of IFS. There were three women – two in IAS and one in IFS. At that time only these two services were given a common foundation course for six months.

Our training school was called Metcalfe House though we did not stay in the main building but in the hutments constructed within the compound during the Second World War. Metcalfe was

---

[4] Asok Mitra, *The New India, 1948-1955: Memoirs of an Indian Civil Servant* (Popular Prakashan, 1991), p. 64

a celebrated officer of the East India Company who served as British Resident to the Mughal Emperor Akbar II (1806-1837) and later acted as the governor-general of India.

*

We were designated as probationers. Each one of us was given a hutment. The living area was separated by a half wall to provide for the bathroom. Four probationers shared one bearer – attendant. My bearer, named William, was a tall, dark and burly fellow with handle-bar moustaches.

The very first morning William filled up the tub with hot water and reported that the bath was ready. Hot water for a bath in May! But I was not sure whether it was mandatory. I quietly poured it out when William was not around and had a normal cold water bath.

Metcalfe House

For the entire batch, it was their first glimpse of the diversity of India. Courses on economics, criminal law, planning, history and culture of India seemed to constitute an extension and widening of our university education. Apart from the principal and vice-principal who were ICS officers, the faculty consisted of two full-time professors – one each for Law and Economics. A good number of lectures were given by top experts from the government and outside. There was a lot of emphasis on rounding off the edges of the callow provincial youth with different regional backgrounds and disparate social extractions. It was astounding to realize how little we knew about India.

The principal, K. Radhakrishnan, was a Tamilian from the Madhya Pradesh cadre. On his deputation to the government of India, he had had a brush with the then home minister, Govind

Ballabh Pant (1887-1961). Having been a veteran freedom fighter, Pant was of the view that the new breed of civil servants should have a '*swadeshi*' orientation. According to him, they should be required to make their own beds, do their own sweeping and washing and possibly also cook on cooperative basis. This would help them develop an empathy with the poor of the country. Radhakrishnan, according to his own account, responded to the proposal somewhat offhandedly by saying, 'Then, Sir, why not send them to district jails?' Pant was not a man to forgive impertinence and had his own way of dealing with the impudent officer. Radhakrishnan did not get his promotion beyond the level of a joint secretary.

Radhakrishnan had a wry and self-deprecating sense of humour. A Tamilian himself, he started with a dig at the prototypical Tamilian accent and pronunciation. He said that if you ask a Tamilian how to spell 'Yes' he would reply, 'yayi' 'yay' 'yes'!

He himself gave lectures once a week and an occasional seminar. He used to scrutinize our compositions and reports and highlight their main points in the class. Once he read out aloud to the whole class a portion from my report after a visit to the Central Tractor Organization. I had given a simile that 'Kans grass, like prostitution, cannot be weeded out.' The whole class laughed at my expense when he said that official reports should not use similes and metaphors but should be plain and matter-of-fact. However, after a few weeks he restored my standing by reading out again from my review of a book as a model of good writing with a touch of subtle humour.

The vice-principal, R.B. Vaghaiwala, was a Parsi officer of the last batch of ICS. About thirty-five, he was full of verve and idealism. No two persons presented a greater contrast than Radhakrishnan and Vaghaiwala. One was a *'sahib'* of the British system, the other a *'sarvodaya'* worker. Though a Parsi, he was steeped in Hinduism and laced his lectures with quotations from the Gita and made us purchase one copy each of Rajaji's book on the Gita.

Vaghaiwala also told us that the motto of our service, namely, *'Yoga Karmasu Kaushalam'*, was derived from the Gita and that we should always keep that in mind. The motto is part of sloka 50 of chapter II. Literally it means that 'Yoga is dexterity in action'. Paraphrased further, it exhorts us to be detached from the results of our action. That promotes selfless action. When you do selfless action you cannot be corrupt. The motto is therefore very aptly chosen for the civil service.

Senior civil servants, eminent political leaders and foreign dignitaries visiting Delhi were invited to the training school for talks followed by question and answers – and dinner. The current probationer, chairman of the mess committee, always asked the last question: 'Shall we rise for dinner, Sir/Madam?' One of the best visitors was Tarlok Singh, an ICS officer who was reputed to be the sole author of India's first Five Year Plan. In his pre-dinner talk he asked us to beware of the trap of developing a sense of complacency for having 'arrived' in life. 'You have reached here by working hard and reading books. Don't give up that practice,' he cautioned, 'otherwise by the time you are thirty-five you will become middle-aged both in body and mind.' I was deeply influenced by that remark and have followed his advice faithfully.

Riding was a mandatory part of our training and we needed to pass an examination in that. Though the hardy jeep had made its entry on the rural scene, there are parts of India which, even now, can be reached only by foot or horseback. Our instructor – an old hand from the Delhi Police – would remark that if one could not control a horse, one would not be able to control a woman! That warning imparted an extra edge to our eagerness to acquire competence in the subject. We wondered whether the warning held the same import for the women probationers. For some of the probationers the weekly visit to the Delhi Police grounds was a white-knuckle experience. J.I., for example, lost his nerve the moment he was helped onto the horseback. Instead of tugging at the reins, he would urge his mount verbally to start. The police horses understood neither Malayalam nor English. He would then complain to the instructor that the horse did not obey. When he tugged at the rein as instructed, the horse shook his head and turned its face to one side. J.I. whined that the horse was trying to bite him.

The morning physical drill also demonstrated a remarkable lack of physical coordination on the part of some of the probationers.

The training schedule also provided for instructions regarding appropriate dress, manners, and modes of communication both verbal and in writing. Probationers were taught that soup was not 'drunk' but 'eaten' and so there should be no slurps while doing so. Also, the soup plates should be tilted not towards, but away from oneself. The proper use of knives and forks was taught by wives of some of the senior officials who spent a few evenings with the trainees and thus earned their dinner while discreetly casting their net for possible catches for their eligible daughters. A retired army officer lectured to us on the fine points of army mess and club etiquette. Another told us how much to tip bearers in restaurants and servants in guest houses. The convention was that the invitation to a guest night covered an eligible daughter, but not a major son. That provided an opportunity for the probationers also to assess the matrimonial 'market'.

Making 'calls' was another point. We were told that calling on other officers would constitute an important part of our old-tie networking. Calling meant dropping in at the residence of colleagues both senior and junior. Visiting cards would be exchanged at the calls. The size of the card and the quality of the paper were laid down. There were to be three cards: one for self which only mentioned the name and service – no academic or other qualifications, and no designation – because the designation would change from time to time while the membership of the service was permanent; the second card – bigger in size – was to carry jointly the names of the officer and spouse; the third card was for the wife exclusively for her use. We all got the first set of cards made from the shop attached to the school. The other two were never needed.

A 'call' would normally result in an invitation for dinner from the called party. The wife of the senior officer herself extended the invitation for dinner through a handwritten note or a phone call to the officer. That was intended to emphasize informality of relationship in the service. Signing the Visitor's Book at the Gate Office of the Raj Bhavan constituted a 'call' on the governor. He would then invite the officer and his spouse to dinner.

This part of the training proved to be largely of historical interest but of doubtful practical use in real life we were to face later on. In practice, hardly any call resulted in any dinner and the visits were seldom returned. As time went by new junior officers seldom called on senior officers. It was explained away by citing rising cost of living because of low salaries and allowances.

A few months into training our allocation to different states was announced. I was allotted to Andhra, a state that had been created about two years earlier, in October 1953. No atlas therefore showed its location and I didn't know whether it was south or north of Madras. Soon, bi-weekly classes were started for teaching the language of the state of allocation. It was then that I learnt that the language of the state was not 'Madrasi' but Telugu. A section officer in the Central Secretariat conducted the language class.

Attached to our school was a 'shop' run by a middle-aged Sindhi refugee called Hari. His young son helped him in the lucrative monopoly. They provided all our needs including instruction in car driving. For that they kept a couple of old Morris Minor jalopies. They were in great demand by the probationers. In most cases, next to the mess bill that was the biggest item of expenditure – except in the case of one and only one probationer, who kept a bicycle for his trips around the city.

After six months, IFS probationers left for their specialized training. IAS probationers spent a fortnight with their batchmates of IPS (Indian Police Service) at their training school, which at that time was located at the charming hill station of Mount Abu in Rajasthan. We were paired up with allottees to our new state in their single rooms. The latter made a return call later in the year. It was aimed at strengthening the spirit of camaraderie. There was also a spell of 'attachment' to a unit of the Indian army for two weeks. Half the batch went to the northeast and the other to Jammu and Kashmir. There we got acquainted with the customs and conventions of the army. We also came to develop a proper appreciation of the hardships under which officers of the armed forces lived and worked. The army attachment was followed by a fortnight's tour of the country called '*Bharat Darshan*'. During that trip we also saw some of the 'temples of modern India', as the first prime minister, Jawaharlal Nehru, used to call the new irrigation and power projects which he had initiated and of which he was so proud.

The last item was a call on the prime minister at his residence, Teen Murti House. Before his arrival from a meeting outside, we had time to go around the public areas of his house. On the wall of gallery at the back of his drawing room on the ground floor hung a row of framed cartoons by the celebrated cartoonist Shankar on Nehru.

After tea, Nehru gave us a gentle talk which was followed by questions by some trainees.

Life at Metcalfe House, though an extension of the university days, gave us a feeling of having arrived. There was no worry of finding a job after the training. On the other hand, we were paid for learning, meeting VIPs and visiting places. Thus groomed, after a year of lectures, visits, seminars and a lot of fun, we were dispatched to our respective states of allotment.

***

Out in the Field

There was a break of fifteen days before we were required to proceed to the states of our allotment. I utilized that to get married to Bindi. It was a simple and sparse affair. On principle we did not take any dowry. That suited the bride's family too because they were in straitened circumstances after the Partition. My father-in-law could not even attend our wedding since he had just found a job in Assam and the fare for commuting to Delhi was too much. His younger brother therefore performed the ceremony. After the wedding, my parents gave a small reception to which I invited my colleagues who were still in Delhi. For my wedding I wore my old white sharkskin suit which had been stitched for Metcalfe House. Because of the garlands with which I was loaded during the wedding ceremony, it became stained. I had therefore no suit to wear for the reception. I borrowed my younger brother Vijay's off-white double-breasted suit which fitted me very well. I kept it for later use and sent it back to him from Visakhapatnam.

Including myself, eight officers were allotted to Andhra: S.K. Singh, K. Subramaniam, V.K. Dar, D. Sankaraguruswamy, K. Balasubhramanyam, V.P. Rama Rao and K.V.V.S. Suryanarayna. The last two belonged to Andhra. Singh resigned after a few years and migrated to the US. Of the other seven, at the time of writing, only I am alive.

We travelled to Kurnool, the capital of Andhra, via Hyderabad. It was an old dilapidated district headquarters of the old Madras Presidency. Our spirits sank at its sight.

The chief secretary O. Pulla Reddy, was an ICS officer who was referred to by all his subordinates as 'The Great Mughal'. He talked to us in his slow measured style while we sat on the edges of our respective chairs before a man who was God to us. In the evening he invited us for tea at his residence where his charming wife and two young daughters were also present. There, Bindi committed a faux pas. Mrs Pulla Reddy was a solicitous hostess. But she was barefoot. For a north Indian, it was unimaginable that a lady in that position would be without footwear. Bindi therefore took her for a maid. But she was very heavily dressed and wore a good deal of jewellery. Foxed, Bindi remarked to one of the girls, 'Your maid is very smart!' The girl replied coolly, 'She is our mother.' When my wife narrated this incident later in the circuit house, all my colleagues agreed that my goose was cooked!

'Your Honour, Sir'

Despite Bindi's verbal indiscretion, the chief secretary told her that since I was the only married officer in the batch he was sending me to the best district in the state – Visakhapatnam.

As the train steamed into the station, a bulky fellow peeped into the window of the compartment shouting: 'Martin Luther, Martin Luther!' I suspected that he must be looking for me and so I popped my head out and waved at him. When I mentioned my name, he saluted me, introduced himself as the tahsildar of the city, and confused me by asking: 'Will the Assistant Collector like some coffee?' I looked around and finding no one except my wife there, asked him, 'Which Assistant Collector?'

'Your Honour, Sir.'

That was my first lesson in protocol. Henceforth I would be addressed by the subordinate officialdom in the third person. I wasn't yet sure whether I should respond in the second person. We got into the front seat of the jeep as he hopped into the back and were driven to the 'circuit house'. It was located on an elevated place with a panoramic view of the harbour and the city. In front of us the Bay of Bengal stretched as far as we could see.

My boss the collector was a genial young officer named N.J. Kamath. His wife Shanti was a smart and equally charming lady. Bindi and I went and called on them in the evening.

Everyone referred to the city as Vizag. In those days it was considered a summer station and so the circuit house was not air-conditioned. The evening breeze from the sea dried up all the perspiration of the day and made it very pleasant.

Vizag was a charming colonial coastal town with an exclusive area called 'uplands', which was slightly higher in elevation and where the collector, the district judge, the vice chancellor of the Andhra University, the chairman of the Port Trust and the pilots of the harbour stayed.

Vegetables like carrots, beans and peas were called 'English' vegetables and were 'imported' from Bangalore.

I was given a cubbyhole in the collectorate as my office. It had a half door which swung in and out. My staff consisted of a camp clerk, an attender and a vacant post with the designation of '*punkha* puller' (punkha is a fan). The attender wore a white dress and a *patta* or a sash across his torso with a metal plate attached to it. I could not go anywhere without him marching ahead of me and clearing the way. The fuss created by my chaperon to herald my arrival embarrassed me very much. He also did not let me carry anything in my hand – not even a sheet of paper. I found it annoying but soon got used to it. The designation of 'punkha puller' was a fiction created to enable me to employ any person of my choice with a skill I fancied. It was good to have some patronage to begin with. We filled that job with a good cook. Though hand-pulled punkhas had disappeared generally, they were still there in some of the *mofussil* areas. We stayed in many a non-descript travellers' bungalow which were appropriately called TBs. They had hand-pulled punkhas. Once we were having a siesta in the TB at Yellamanchali while a poor old man pulled the punkha from outside the room. A sudden gust of wind flung open the door providing a view of a young honeymooning couple to the man, which must have been a good recompense to his tired eyes.

Roaming the District

My district training started with the revenue department. For that training which lasted a month I was sent to Yellamanchali – a *taluk* about thirty kilometres from the headquarters. I started with village officers. There were two of them – *karnam* (called *patwari* in the north), and headman. The karnam maintained about twenty registers which carried the basic statistics of the village.

He wielded considerable power for mischief through the manipulation of records. The headman was the ceremonial head of the village much like my grandfather had been in his times. At that time both these posts were hereditary and I was advised to be courteous to them. From them I learnt the difference between rice and paddy; what paddy looked like, how it differed from other crops, and how one could visually estimate the extent of a field and predict the quality of the crop.

Thence I progressed to revenue inspector and then to tahsildar. In between the collector occasionally took me on tours with him where I saw how he did his work, received petitions and disposed of them. He also gave me oral explanations and instructions about the intricacies of various aspects of his job.

For a fortnight I acted as district treasury officer. Two accounts were maintained for all the money in the treasury – one for the Government of India and one for the State Government. I had to put my signatures beside hundreds of entries a day in a register which showed deposits and withdrawals. That exercise helped me firm up my signature, which has altered little since.

While staying at Yellamanchali, Bindi and I used to go for a stroll on the main road after our early dinner. We noticed that a number of men and women squatting on both sides of the road in the darkness of the evening would get up on seeing us passing by them. For quite some time we believed that it was out of respect for us, and I wondered how so many people had come to recognize us in such a small place. One day I told the tahsildar to advise them not to inconvenience themselves because of us. The tahsildar was embarrassed in having to explain to me that they were actually answering the call of nature on the roadside and got up on seeing us out of modesty. As soon as we had passed by they would resume their interrupted call. After that enlightenment we stopped our evening constitutional.

I also trained with other district officers of forest, education, P.W.D. and the like.

Soon, I also started my magisterial work. To begin with, I was designated magistrate of the third class, which empowered me to try cases entailing a punishment of one month's imprisonment and/or a fine of one hundred rupees. Before being let loose, I had spent a week training with the district and sessions judge. Prohibition – a hangover from Madras – was in force in Andhra at that time, and my first case was a prohibition offence. According to rules, unless the High Court gave special exemption, the evidence of witnesses was to be recorded in the regional language. Since the permission had not come before the start of my judicial work, I had to record the statements of the witnesses in Telugu. As I wrote laboriously in Telugu, my camp clerk stood behind me looking down over my shoulders and correcting my spellings. Having recorded the evidence, I did not find it easy to decipher it later. There again my camp clerk came to my rescue. The lawyers argued in English and so that part was easy. At the end of my first case, I could not make up my mind whether the accused was guilty or not and I did not want to punish an innocent person. So, after the conclusion of arguments, I called the public prosecutor aside and asked him: 'Off the record, tell me if the accused is really guilty.'

The old bandicoot, clad in a white shirt and dhoti, black coat and lawyers' collar, put me down with his impassive reply: 'Your Honour, I am doing my duty. You are doing your duty. God alone knows the truth.'

I had never consulted God before and didn't know how to do that. Anyway, it was too small a matter to disturb Him. The public prosecutor's snub boosted my confidence. I awarded the maximum punishment within my gift and sent the accused to jail. He showed no emotion.

Three months later I became a second class magistrate. Six more months were to elapse before I became a first class magistrate. That was something. But since judiciary had been separated from the executive after the promulgation of the Constitution in 1950, collectors and sub-collectors were permitted to exercise magisterial powers only relating to law and order.

*

The sleepy city of Vizag had just started waking up to development. It was the eastern headquarters of the Indian Navy and a shipyard had been established. The Caltex Oil Company had set up an oil refinery and the Coromandel Fertilizer Factory was also coming up. The Waltair Club was next to the circuit house and the collector was its ex-officio president. At that time Vizag also served as the summer headquarters of the governor of Andhra since compared to Kurnool it was coolness itself. Araku Valley and Chintapalle tribal areas were about 800 metres in altitude and were quite cool in summer. The rate of travelling and daily allowance was fifty per cent higher. It was doubly good to tour there.

The buses in Vizag had long wooden benches for the passengers. We found it strange that if Bindi and I boarded a local bus the entire bench was vacated for the two of us and even the university students would not sit beside us in spite of our invitation. Such was the awe in which IAS officers were held in the districts!

I was less than six months into training when the new and enlarged state of Andhra Pradesh was created on 1 November 1956. What the leaders had fought for so long in vain, my arrival resolved in a short time! We suddenly felt personally enriched because Hyderabad became the capital of the new state. It was a beautiful city and we saw glimpses of its grandeur during our bi-annual trips to it for our departmental examinations.

One of the important items of training for us was revenue settlement. It is the basis of the system on which the land revenue assessment of villages is fixed. The origin of the system is attributed to Todar Mall, Emperor Akbar's revenue minister. But the permanent demand system (of revenue) was one of the reforms made by the British during the period of Lord Cornwallis as governor-general. Before that land was farmed out to the highest bidder. That person in turn squeezed the cultivator as much as he could. Not knowing when the revenue demand would be increased, the cultivator did not make any permanent improvement in his holding.

Untouchability

The one-month settlement training was under a state civil service officer promoted to IAS. Though the settlement officer was equal in rank to collector, he did not enjoy the same prestige in the public eye. D. Basavaraju, the settlement officer, let no opportunity pass to mention that he enjoyed collector's rank. His letterhead proclaimed: 'Collector-grade Settlement Officer.' He was past fifty and was stationed at Nuzvid, a taluk of the Krishna district. It had been a zamindar's estate before the abolition of the feudal system. All the seven assistant collectors were sent there together and lodged in the ex-zamindar's mansion.

We stayed on the first floor of the house. A big hall on the same floor with three or four holes in the floor served as the bathroom. We had to squat on the holes to answer the call of nature. In time we heard a thud when the matter fell about twenty feet on the floor below. The output was removed by a low-caste 'untouchable' servant. That was the first time I saw the practice of untouchability incorporated into the architecture of a house.

One day Basavaraju invited us to lunch. It was arranged in the open in the shade of a tree. When the fare had been spread out, I got up and started to help myself as one does in a buffet. Basavaraju interrupted me and said, 'What you have done is not correct. Let my man serve you.' I was taken aback by the snub. It was explained later by my colleagues that he was an orthodox Brahmin and that I, a non-Brahmin (and presumably a Christian), had contaminated the food by touching it.

We were taken from place to place and were taught how to determine various types of soil which were graded into eight categories. We would be asked to pick up a handful of soil and name what type it belonged to. We learnt the distinction between dry and irrigated lands. We were also taught how to determine in advance the likely yield of a standing crop. Some lands were single crop, while others were double crop. All these and more went into the determination of the land revenue 'demand' from the cluster of villages which was done annually at a week-long visit. It was called '*jamabandi*' – one of the many Persian terms found in the Indian land revenue system.

There was a dilapidated jeep for taking us around. None of us had driven a jeep before and everyone was keen to drive it around. It was therefore decided that pushing the driver to the back seat, each of us would drive it by turns. One day, Sankaraguruswamy swerved the jeep to save some animal. In that process, he lost control and the jeep fell into a ditch by the roadside and overturned. All of us were injured in varying degrees and were rushed to the district hospital. Most of us suffered minor injuries but Suryanarayana fractured his leg and spent three months in bed.

In a Cinema Hall

One day we learnt that a Hindi picture had come to the local cinema house. We went eagerly to see the film. Some half an hour after the picture started, it came to a sudden stop. In the stalls below us we heard someone hectoring in Telugu. We thought some trouble had erupted. Our Andhra colleagues told us not to worry. The man was an employee of the cinema house. He was explaining to the spectators the story so far and giving a glimpse of what was going to happen next. This was done because people did not know enough of Hindi. We were greatly amused by this ingenious practice.

We also saw a Telugu picture later. Our Andhra colleagues whispered simultaneous translation of the dialogues to us. It lasted more than three hours.

It was recommended that as soon as possible, the trainee assistant collector should buy a car for touring. Travelling allowance (TA) and daily allowance (DA) covered the running expenses adequately. The government gave a loan equivalent to eight months' salary which worked out to Rs 3,200. The price of a new Hindustan car was Rs 10,000. All of us started looking out for used cars.

Nizam's Car

During one of my visits to Hyderabad for departmental exams, I bought a 1946 model Humber Hawk car which had once belonged to the Seventh Nizam. A bomb was thrown at it unsuccessfully in 1946. With its long nose, low clearance, leather upholstery, teak panelling and a clock, it had a most aristocratic look. The damage to the body had been repaired but its brakes were yet to be fixed properly. I was so smitten by its pedigree and beauty that I could not wait. The price was easily brought down to my limit of Rs 3,200.

God knows why I did not have any accident driving it to Vizag. Soon I found that it was too heavy on petrol and the more I ran it and the more travelling allowance I earned, the more financial loss I sustained. I therefore started regretting my purchase.

As a trainee assistant collector, I was required to read various manuals on local laws, Fundamental Rules, Accounts Manual, old tattered tomes containing 'standing orders' of the Board of Revenue littered with correction slips, and also acquire proficiency in Telugu.

We were required to pass departmental examinations in the subjects mentioned above. The exams were held once every six months at the state capital, Hyderabad.

I was required to submit a weekly diary of my activities and reading of manuals to the collector. He, in turn, reviewed it and submitted it to the Board of Revenue at Hyderabad. I didn't know whether a short diary would impress the collector or a long diary full of details. We consulted our colleagues whenever an opportunity occurred and found that it depended on the respective collector's point of view. On the whole it was safer to submit a detailed diary so that an impression was created that I was a serious learner.

Pongal is celebrated as the harvest festival in Andhra Pradesh. Our first harvest of love came on the Pongal day of 12 January 1957 in the form of a nine-pounder boy exactly nine months after our marriage. We named him Rahul after Gautama Buddha's son. However, in the style of the state and by way of fun we also gave him the name of 'Narendra Visakhapatnam Pongal Rao', shortened as N.V. Pongal Rao. Somehow it caught on. The dictionary meaning of the term 'Pongal' is 'boiling over'. Our Pongal Rao had the temper to match that.

Proficiency in the state language Telugu was also subjected to an examination. A senior officer once told us that the best way to learn a language was to keep a mistress who spoke that language. Some officers had tried it successfully earlier. The next best was to mix well with the speakers of the language. The first option had been foreclosed by my marriage. The *huzur sheristedar* (chief superintendent) of the collector, out of consideration for me, had made sure that the small staff posted for me knew Hindi. The result was that while I made little progress in Telugu, their competence in Hindi improved vastly. Officials always spoke in English. I therefore found that I was not making adequate progress in Telugu. I tried to make up by engaging a tutor and for that purpose I asked my camp clerk Chittibabu to request the headmaster of the local high school at Yellamanchali to see me. Then I turned aside to Bindi and suggested that she should arrange for some snacks and tea for the meeting.

The next day I asked Chittibabu whether he had talked to the headmaster. 'Yes, Sir,' he said confidently, 'I have sent a letter to him, and he is coming.' I said there was no need to send a letter. He replied, 'No, Sir, that makes sure that he gets the message.' Pronto, he produced a copy of the letter from his file. I was both embarrassed and amused to see its contents:

Dear Sir,
I am directed by the Assistant Collector to ask you to see him at 4.30 p.m. at his bungalow tomorrow.
Tea will be served.

Yours faithfully,
K. Chittibabu

The letter was rather peremptory in tone and the declaration that tea would be served sounded pompous. Also, calling our ramshackle rented house a 'bungalow' was a big joke even for us. It leaked during rains and we had constantly to shift our beds at night during rainfall. The headmaster came in the evening and suggested the name of one of his teachers as a tutor for me. But that did not work out.

Examinations

While I flunked in some of the subjects, I caused a flutter amongst my batchmates by passing the language test in the first shot.

A bundle of some typical petitions submitted to collectors on their visits or annual inspections used to be given to the trainee officers. They started with elaborate openings like, '*Maharaj, Raj Sri, Dora garu, Collector garu* ...' and then prayed either for the remission of revenue due to drought or made some other request. We memorized the first few lines of these. In the oral exams by the time we rattled off two or three lines, it was taken for granted that we knew the rest.

The miracle in my case happened because my examiner was an ICS officer, M.T. Raju, whose reputation was as tough as his interior was soft. Having noted my fluent reading of the petition, he asked me if I could count in Telugu. He heard me count up to twenty and stopped me there. After all, under the Indian penal law a person who cannot count up to twenty is defined as an idiot. I had proved in Telugu that I was not one.

Then he announced ominously: 'I shall ask you questions in English and you must reply in Telugu.' I shivered, waiting for him to shoot.

'What is your name?' he asked in English.

'Narendra Luther, *andi*,' I replied in Telugu.

'*Andi*' means 'please'.

'Father's name?'

I knew that too.

'Where do you come from?'

'Punjab – Pakistan, *andi*,' I elaborated.

'Which district are you posted to?'

'Visakhapatnam, *andi*,' I replied fluently in Telugu astutely avoiding its Anglicized version – Vizag.

Raju shook my hand as he got up. I had passed.

At that time all matters involving finance were dealt with by the A.G. (accountant general). Even the monthly travelling allowance bills were scrutinized and passed by the office of the A.G. Once there was inordinate delay in the case of one of my bills. I sent many reminders and received no response. Hard-pressed financially, and annoyed, I sent an official telegram to the A.G. It elicited an immediate response. It did not refer to the point I had raised. Instead, it pointed out that I was remiss in using public funds for a private matter by sending an official telegram. It therefore asked me to remit the cost of the telegram to the treasury and report compliance. The system was reformed many years later thus removing a constant irritant.

The period of district training lasted eighteen months. In November 1957 I was posted as sub-collector to Gudur division of Nellore district. In Andhra Pradesh, as in the old Madras Presidency, selected divisions of districts are earmarked for IAS officers. They have an official bungalow.

The current rule pertaining to transfer allowed me to carry a carriage with two horses in a railway wagon. On a representation to the government, a G.O. (government order) was issued relaxing the rule and allowing me to carry a car instead. This sort of thing happened on every transfer for some more time till someone in the secretariat had the courage to amend the rule.

*

At Vizag I read the two-volume charming history of the ICS – *Men who Ruled India* by a former ICS officer who had used the pen name Philip Woodruff. The first volume is titled 'The Founders' and the second, 'The Guardians'. It highlights not only their contribution to the basic work of laying the foundation of an impartial administration, but also underscores the contribution made by ICS officers to Indian studies as pointed out earlier.

I was fascinated by the book and the versatility of some of my service forebears. That reinforced my earlier resolve of emulating those who went beyond the confines of their official duties.

* * *

Early Renown

I was posted to Gudur division in Nellore district, a town with a population of about 30,000. It lay on the grand trunk railway route and was one of the biggest railway stations in India. All trains to Chennai stopped there for a good half an hour. The number of trains passing through it was so large that the level crossing gate near Nayudupet was closed most of the day. Sometimes it took about an hour of waiting before it opened for a few minutes. The mica belt around Gudur was considered to be the second biggest in India and there were a good number of mica barons in town.

My official residence was in a plot of about three acres of unfenced land. A short drive led to the front of the house which had a small circular lawn. It was a double-storey colonial bungalow. The ground floor of the house had the drawing room, dining room, kitchen, pantry and the bungalow office which opened on to the east side. The three bedrooms were upstairs which were approached by a wooden staircase. I counted some fifty windows, two garages and a row of servants' quarters at a respectable distance from the house. There was a huge tree in front of the bungalow office. The petitioners would start gathering under its shade in the morning. The gentry were accommodated in the veranda or in the sparsely furnished drawing room according to the discretion of my *daffadar*.

The house did not have any plumbing. There was no running water and so the bathroom did not have any tap or flush system. A servant filled up the drum in the bathrooms with enough water before we woke up.

There was a chamber pot which was cleared twice a day by a *yanadi* – a tribal servant. At first I thought it was his name. When we asked him he gave us his real name and he was greatly pleased when we started calling him by his name Chandra instead of yanadi.

My daily routine was to sit in the bungalow office at nine in the morning by when my camp clerk would already be present. For two hours I met petitioners and went through *tappal* – official mail – and disposed of some important files. The office in the town opened at eleven am. A police station was attached to the office and I had often to walk the thirty odd steps to it for receiving a phone call. I held my court twice a week.

The house was partly electrified and did not have a phone. Some predecessors of mine had devised a formula under which each succeeding tenant would electrify a part of the house and recover half the charges from his successor on his transfer. Accordingly, I electrified a part of the house of the first floor so that we could sleep under a fan at night.

In a far corner of the compound of my bungalow was the club. I was its ex-officio president. It offered facilities for tennis, billiards, badminton and cards. Some leading mica barons of the town were its members. Whenever I was in station I would go there and play tennis. I learnt billiards there from the marker. Bindi was the only lady member and she played some badminton. Most of the other members played cards and some tennis. There were two young Anglo-Indians named Freddie and Maxie, former officers in the Royal Indian Air Force, working as agents of the importers of mica. They were very lively and used to regale members with their anecdotes. I later used one of their personal experiences with the Nizam's legendary parsimony in my book on Hyderabad.

Returning from the club we had our bath, an early dinner and thereafter retired upstairs. Only Chandra, the Yanadi, was privileged to come upstairs.

Halts and Marches

I was required to tour my division for fifteen days in a month. In order to ensure that one did not make any superficial and hurried trips, the rules laid down that there should be one 'halt' for two 'marches'. A 'halt' was defined as a stay for a night preceded and followed by a 'march'. 'March' was the day of commuting one way or the other. While the ratio between 'halts' and 'marches' could vary in the short run, over a period of six months, it had to conform to the formula.

I was required to submit fortnightly diary of my work and tours which was reviewed by the collector and the Board of Revenue.

We carried most of our equipment and rations in the boot of the car and the meal was cooked there by the cook who travelled with us – or sometimes by my wife. Often we had an early dinner at home and then made a 'march' to our camp for the first 'halt'. This wasn't much of a trouble because there was no place which was more than two hours' drive from my headquarters. There were three taluks in my charge. One of them was Venkatagiri, a former estate well known for handloom saris. There we enjoyed a stay in a fully equipped suite of the old mansion of the former raja. The extent of exploitation under the feudal system can be gauged from the fact that the raja had a palace, a polo playground, a stable of horses, besides jewellery and other items, but no high school. And yet in territory and revenue, it qualified only for a small taluk under my charge.

SHAR's birthplace

One day I made a trip to a far-off godforsaken place known as Sriharikota. It was an island in the backwaters of the Bay of Bengal and was sparsely inhabited by a tribe called Yanadi – to which our own Yanadi servant belonged. Very few sub-collectors had visited the place. I drove to the furthest point by car and then boarded a country boat for the slow overnight sail. I slept while the boat was quietly rowed. Early next morning I was woken up by the noise of drum-beating. This was made by a group of tribals to welcome me. The village elders greeted me with flowers and coconuts. I walked about 300 metres with dancing and singing tribals and reached a derelict travellers' bungalow. There was not much work except to talk to the islanders, listen to their simple problems and give them some assurance. After a campfire in the evening I had dinner and got ready to retire in the boat which was rowed back to the mainland. It was considered a mosquito-infested place and I was much commended for taking the bold step of visiting it. Now Sriharikota is the headquarters of SHAR – Sriharikota High Altitude Range – and is no longer an island. It is a high-security area. I have not visited the place since then, but prime ministers and presidents often do. In my time rocket science was really rocket science. How did they come to select the place for space research?

The Deluge

I had been in Gudur only for a few weeks when one day it started raining heavily. It rained incessantly for four days and nights. It was well past midnight when I received a police wireless message from the government. Two trains, the Madras Mail and the G.T. Express (as they were then called), were held up in my jurisdiction near Nayudupet and Sulurpet respectively and I was asked to arrange necessary relief to stranded passengers and other inhabitants in the affected areas. I sent a message to the deputy superintendent of police, Ramakota Reddy, who stayed close by and we decided to leave early in the morning. My wife had gone home for a holiday.

We had barely gone out of town when we found the national highway under waist-deep water as far as we could see. No vehicle could go further. Everybody looked on helplessly and suggested that we return. That was not an option. I sent my car back and proceeded to wade through the water which gradually reached my chest. Others had to follow suit. After crossing the breach, we got hold of a lorry stalled on the other side and drove up to Nayudupet. There we met some of the local officials who briefed us about the situation around the area. Railway officers were busy repairing the breached railway track.

Our first priority was to provide succour to about 500 passengers of the stranded trains. The tahsildar at Nayudupet had adequate quantity of rice and *sambhar* cooked and we carried it in huge utensils on railway trolleys loaned by the railway officers.

When we started serving food to the passengers, some amusing incidents occurred. There was a wedding party from Rajasthan in a compartment. They spurned rice and sambhar offered by us and said that they would eat only rotis made with jaggery. I told them that this was not a feast but an emergency and our aim was to save them from starvation. A young man from Delhi protested that there was no sweet dish with the meals! There were enough starving persons in the train who were grateful for our help and I ordered that those who declined the meagre succour should be ignored till they came crying for help.

The next destination was Sulurpet, a taluk headquarters and a railway station about fifteen kilometres away. We covered that distance on bicycles which we commandeered from the village. Luckily, the train there was stranded at the railway station.

The magnitude of the floods was so great that in one single night fifty-one persons were washed away by the river Swarnamukhi. It had overflowed into various tanks causing a chain of breached tanks. At places, the water level had risen on the national highway to a height of twenty-one feet. People were arriving in hordes from the affected villages to Sulurpet. I ordered the schools closed and set up refugee camps there. I asked the officials to buy rice and other essential commodities needed by the refugees. Some of them, particularly women, also needed some clothes. When the tahsildar went to buy rice in the market, the merchants raised the price. I thereupon instructed the tahsildar to seize all the stocks available with shopkeepers and to issue written receipts to them. We would pay them later. We also bought enough saris and dhotis from the market and had them distributed to those affected. To my shock, those saris and dhotis found their way back to the market the next day. The beneficiaries had sold them at half the price and made money out of their relief supplies.

Meanwhile, the railway officials had been busy repairing the tracks at an impressive speed. By evening trains were ready to start.

However, our task of relief and rehabilitation of the affected villagers was long drawn out.

A few days later the district superintendent of police, Anandram, also arrived on the scene. That added to the zeal of the local police force in its assistance in the relief work.

I had not been able to bring even a change of clothes with me. So I borrowed a pair of dhoti and kurta from the tahsildar which I used as nightwear. Representatives of different organizations like the Ramakrishna Mission and others also started pouring in to contribute to the relief work. We converted the travellers' bungalow into a dormitory and all of us slept there on the floor.

Police to meet you!

My sister was to come to visit me from Delhi according to a prior programme. She had small children with her and was visiting the south for the first time. I could not go to the Gudur railway station to receive her, so I sent a sub-inspector of police with a note to her explaining the position.

The sight of a policeman instead of her brother at a new place made her nervous. The sub-inspector reassured her and gave her my note. She got down most reluctantly.

By then the situation had improved and the collector was able to reach Sulurpet. The venerable old gentleman, Mohibulla had risen from the ranks and was a very gentle person indeed. He was pleasantly surprised to see the arrangements and was so overcome with emotion that he embraced me and complimented me profusely.

After some time, the chief minister and ministers started visiting the flood-affected area and it was heartening to note that everywhere people praised my work. One local Telugu paper published ballads about me and called me '*devudu*' – a god.

After the whole operation was over, the government issued a gazette extraordinary notification placing on record the government's appreciation of the flood relief work done by Anandram and me at risk to our lives.

I became a celebrity; newspapers published my pictures and the statements of various ministers praising my work.

Quirky Seniors

One day Subramaniam, the second member of the Board of Revenue, came on an official visit to Nellore, the district headquarters. The new collector, V. Srinivasachari, invited him for dinner and invited me to join them. Next morning, Subramanian called me and said that he would like to give a present to the collector's daughter in return for the dinner he had given him, so that he did not remain under any obligation to him. He asked me what the cost of dinner would be insofar as he was concerned. I said since in any case the dinner would have been cooked for the collector and his family, the cost in respect of Subramaniam could only be calculated on the basis of marginal costing. He observed that a good meal cost two rupees in any restaurant. Since it was better than a restaurant meal, and there was a sweet dish also, it should be about three-and-a-half rupees. I readily endorsed that figure. He then asked me to accompany him to the bazaar to help him select some suitable gift for a girl of four to five years of age that should cost three and-a-half rupees. We went round the bazaar and found nothing which cost exactly that amount and the big boss would not consider spending a paisa more or less. Ultimately, fed up, I signalled to the tahsildar to suggest to the shopkeeper to accept that amount for a doll for which he had earlier quoted five rupees on the understanding that

I would pay the difference later. I then sought the venerable senior's advice whether I too should also pay off the collector for my dinner. Subramaniam allayed my conscience by clarifying that only the superior officer came under the convention. The junior officer was entitled to the senior's hospitality.

Later, Subramaniam came to Gudur for the annual inspection of my office. Going through the draft notes of inspection prepared by his advance office party, suddenly, Subramaniam raised his head, gave me a five-rupee note and asked me to send someone to get a comb and a small mirror which he had forgotten to bring with him. He declined my offer of lending him my set for the duration of his stay. A clerk was sent on the errand. He returned soon with the items and a receipt for the amount and said the change of 75 paise would be coming soon. Subramaniam got busy with the inspection, but after about five minutes muttered suddenly: 'What about the change?' I thought he had found some fault in the register. I asked: 'What change, Sir?' The tahsildar understood the point and submitted humbly that the person was on the way. Thereupon Subramaniam reverted to his scrutiny. Not five minutes had elapsed when again he looked up and asked impatiently: 'I say, what happened to the change?' The tahsildar got up and submitted: 'Sir, he should be coming any moment.' It was less than five minutes again when Subramaniam asked with considerable agitation: 'What is happening? Where has he gone to get the change?' Fortunately, an attender appeared just then and respectfully handed over the change to him. There was relief all around. Subramaniam then resumed his scrutiny of the records in peace.

While on this subject I would like to mention the instance of Unnithan, who was the first member of the Board of Revenue. He came to Gudur for official inspection and seeing that the revenue minister, Kala Vekatarao, was staying in one room of the travellers' bungalow, he asked for a Swiss Cottage tent to be fixed for his stay in the compound of the taluk office next door. The tahsildar and his staff were hard put to locating the tent because it had not been used for years after the travellers' bungalow had been built. Finally, they got hold of it, dusted it and then erected it. By that time, Unnithan, on the advice of the minister, had changed his mind and decided to stay in one of the rooms of the guesthouse.

Later in the afternoon, he called me to say that he had to return to Hyderabad immediately for an emergency and wanted me to arrange a vehicle for him to go to Chennai from where he could take a flight to Hyderabad. I did so and asked if everything was alright.

He replied that he had asked for an appointment with the chief minister for a courtesy call and his office informed him over the police wireless that the chief minister's office had given him the appointment the next day. I ventured to suggest that since he was on tour, a request could be made for another day. He said it would be a discourtesy to the chief minister and so he must keep the appointment. It struck me as odd to leave important work just for a courtesy call, but I could not go beyond a point.

Unnithan not only reached on time but also told the chief minister how he had rushed back to keep the appointment. Sanjeeva Reddy, who was the chief minister, pulled him up severely for a lack of sense of balance.

Muslims in the south speak Urdu in a peculiar accent which is difficult for people from the north to understand. Once I invited my collector, Mohibulla, for dinner. The genial old man started conversing with my sister who sat next to him. After a while, my sister said to him, 'Excuse me, but I don't understand Telugu.' Mohibulla clarified in embarrassment, 'But I was speaking to you in Urdu!'

One sizzling summer morning we got up from bed soaked in perspiration. I cursed the heat of Gudur and prayed for some relief. At that moment Chandra, the Yanadi, brought a telegram from the chief secretary informing me that I was selected for training in community development at Mussoorie for six weeks. I was asked to proceed immediately. That was a miracle.

An Arduous Job

On my return from training in October 1958, I was transferred to Hyderabad as under secretary (political) in the general administration department.

Luckily, the job carried with it a designated house, though it was in a colony called Irram Manzil which was poorly built and provided amenities of a very low order. However, it was a blessing to have a ready roof over our head in a city like Hyderabad.

It is funny that the secretariat jobs carry a special pay (at that time) of Rs 200 by reason of the 'arduous nature' of the duties involved. In fact, they are cushy compared to field jobs. The fiction is created by civil servants to compensate themselves for the loss of TA and DA which helps them maintain the car in field postings.

My job carried an additional special allowance of sixty rupees because it involved protocol work. That subsidy for clothing was a legacy from the old Madras state.

I was in charge of the division which dealt with all confidential matters, political affairs and protocol, and controlled the two premier services viz., IAS and IPS. I reported to a deputy secretary named B.R.K. Sastry. He was an intelligent, pleasant and informal person and, in his turn, reported to M.P. Pai, the chief secretary. Pai was a handsome and sophisticated man with social graces including a good sense of humour. He and his wife became very fond of me and our family which caused considerable heartburn to many colleagues.

Right at the beginning Sastry gave me a piece of advice: 'Don't initiate any note yourself. Ask one of your subordinates to put up a note in accordance with your ideas on the subject. That way, you will never be held directly responsible for anything going wrong. In that case you would be able to plead that you were misled.' I did not agree with him and entertained a loftier idea of my responsibilities. However, his advice was well meant and I found that most senior officers followed that course.

One of my main jobs was to scrutinize the intelligence report of the police and the daily summary of news and editorial opinions sent by the department of information and public relations.

On the basis of these inputs, I had to prepare a fortnightly draft letter as from the chief secretary to the Union home secretary. All chief secretaries sent similar letters and all were put together and further summarized. The final summary constituted the situation report on the country and was put up to the home minister and the prime minister. This practice was a continuation of the Mughal system. Mughal emperors used to sign the daily summary of reports received from different parts of the empire every evening before retiring.

There was still considerable informality at the highest level. The chief minister had only one private secretary of the rank of deputy superintendent of police. We called him to check if the CM was free and, if so, would walk into his office whenever necessary.

I was generally present at all high-level meetings and official functions including protocol and entertainment by the chief minister. Consequently that brought me in frequent interaction with the chief minister.

Prime Minister Nehru used to write regular monthly letters to chief ministers of all states. In those letters he tried to bring to the notice of the chief ministers some aspects of national and international situation, and some of the concerns which needed to be addressed. It was like a gentle patriarch addressing his family on national and international issues. At that time the Congress party ruled both at the Centre and the states – except for Kerala which for some time had a Communist government. Therefore, though the Constitution of India was federal, with one party ruling all but one state, and given Nehru's towering personality, it virtually became a unitary system.

Head of Department

The department of information and public relations of the Hyderabad State was depleted by its trifurcation in 1956. The state of Andhra had no such department.

I was pleasantly surprised when in September 1959 I was promoted and asked to build up the department of information and public relations.

*

I had hardly settled in my new job when our joy was redoubled with the birth of a daughter on 28 October 1959. That completed our family in accordance with the prevalent norms of family planning. We named her Sandhya – meaning twilight, the time to pray.

In contrast to Rahul's fiery temper, she was cool as a cucumber and has retained that trait right through.

*

Turning to my job, I proceeded to study the working of the information and broadcasting ministry of the government of India and some of the departments of information in the major states, and prepared a plan for a reorganization and enlargement of the existing setup. I took the file for discussion with my minister, P. Ranga Reddy. After a brief discussion, he picked up the file and took me across the corridor to the finance minister, K. Brahamananda Reddy. I explained the main features of my proposals and both of them signed the file then and there. Thus the massive reorganization of the department entailing creation of many new jobs and enhancing the pay scales of other officials was done in a jiffy. The finance secretary took objection to the bypassing of the finance department but was overruled.

It was a tough job to enforce work culture amongst the staff. I forbade officers from coming late and from chewing paan at my meetings. It was a common practice in Hyderabad so much so that a spittoon was part of the official furnishing and appurtenances provided to every secretary and head of department.

I picked some bright officers and took special interest in their development. Some of them responded to new challenges and grew in stature. Out of all of them the most outstanding was C.V. Narasimha Reddy. He was a callow youth from the back of beyond of the rural areas of Nalgonda. But by stages he developed so much that in course of time he retired as director of the department.

After his retirement he earned a PhD in public relations – probably the first in India. Thereafter he became a professor of the subject in the Open University and lectured in many universities abroad. He started a quarterly journal, *P. R. Voice*, which he is still editing at eighty-three.

The department took new initiatives in areas it had never touched before.

The monthly journal of the government was known as a rag picked up free by the public because it sold well to scrap dealers. It was crude in its content and behind its schedule by months because the government's press where it was printed gave it no importance. I took it out of the government press, diversified its contents by adding literary features, banned the publication of ministers' photographs, and improved its get-up. Handsome payments were made to contributors to the literary section of the journal. As a result, the magazine started picking up and ultimately it reached a paid circulation figure of 37,000 which was a record in the whole country.

Nehru in an Ad

An interesting incident occurred during a visit of Prime Minister Jawaharlal Nehru in November 1959. At the Nagarjunasagar Dam, which was then under construction, one of the thousands of workers taking headloads of mortar up the bamboo scaffolding stopped and, looking admiringly at Nehru, said in Telugu: '*Idi meere velinginchina deepam.*' The chief minister, Sanjeeva Reddy, translated it for Nehru: 'It is a lamp lighted by you.' Nehru was touched by such a poetic expression by an illiterate labourer. He quietly scribbled it in Roman on a piece of paper. In his speech to a huge public meeting at Vijayawada the next morning, he used this expression in Telugu to a thunderous applause.

I decided to make use of this incident and issued an advertisement with Nehru's picture. The headline of the ad was: 'Nehru Speaks Telugu.' The body line contained a summary of the incident and the baseline said that such new lamps were being lit all over the country.

After about a fortnight I got a letter from the prime minister's office informing me that the prime minister did not like his photograph to be used in advertisements.

That was the standard then. Contrast it with what is happening now!

Let me narrate another incident here. During those days when there were Congress governments in most states, the Congress party used to hold its annual session in some state or the other on a grand scale. All the state government departments were asked to put up stalls in the exhibitions for which they paid rent and incurred other expenditure. Advertisements were also given for the souvenir published on the occasion. Needless to say the Congress party made good money from such sessions. In 1963 the Communist party held its annual session in Vijayawada and invited government departments for similar participation. Predictably, it drew no response from any department. However, I accepted the invitation. This 'act of betrayal' was reported to Chief Minister K. Brahamananda Reddy. He called me and asked why I was participating in the exhibition organized by the Communist party. I replied: 'Sir, if I were the head of the Communist party I would not have allowed any government department to enter the exhibition. Now that the "enemy" is inviting me to propagate under its very nose, I should not miss the opportunity.' Brahamananda Reddy smiled and said that that angle hadn't occurred to him.

My spell in the department also enabled me to revive my interest in writing which had been in abeyance for the last six years. Hyderabad is an 'Urdu city' and I wrote frequently in that language. I also revived my old interest in radio and became a regular broadcaster. My first book of fiction and humour in Urdu was published in 1964.

I had an unusually long tenure of five years in the department. I thus served four chief ministers and five ministers. Amongst the ministers that I enjoyed working with most was P.V. Narasimha Rao. That was his first stint as a minister and he was, as ministers go, rather young – about thirty-six years old. He was a very learned person and knew a number of languages. In spite of all that he was most informal. I could argue about any issue with him. He never forced any decision on me.

One evening when we were returning from Warangal to Hyderabad in the same car, he suddenly broke into a plaintive Hindi song. I too instinctively started tapping my thighs to the rhythm of the song. When the spell broke after some time, I was bold enough to say in jest, 'Sir, we should give a public performance together!' He smiled disarmingly.

Incidentally, I heard the first *jugalbandi*[5] between Carnatic and Hindustani classical music that he organized at his house for an exclusive gathering.

During Nehru's visit to the state in November 1959, at my suggestion he was chosen to interpret Nehru's speeches from English to Telugu. During the very first speech at Shadnagar, an interesting incident occurred. Nehru had just opened his speech with his usual 'Friends and Comrades' when Narasimha Rao proceeded to render it into Telugu. Nehru waved his hand imperiously at him and said, 'O, shut up. Let me finish my sentence.' This snub was carried over the public address system and we heard a snigger rising from the audience much to Narasimha Rao's discomfiture.

---

[5] Jugalbandi is a fusion of two or more artists playing together on different instruments. It is also done between two different systems of music – Western and Hindustani. It was made popular internationally by Ravi Shankar and Yehudi Menuhin in the late twentieth century

Tourism as a separate subject did not exist in the state and when the government of India emphasized its importance, it was tagged on to the information department.

I prepared the basic outline for the development of tourism and initiated many projects.

All in all, it was a very exciting and rewarding experience to build up a department from scratch. More so was the appreciation I received all around including some of those who later on became ministers and chief ministers, a prime minister and another, president of India.

The Urban Bride

It was also the time that I embarked upon my journey of discovery of the beautiful city of Hyderabad and began savouring its truly cosmopolitan culture.

Located on a plateau at an average altitude of 1700 feet, the city had numerous lakes in and around it. Its greenery and small number of cars kept the ambient temperature of the city low. The best season was monsoon which was decreed to break on 7 June. Sometimes when it didn't, the deviation was apologetically explained by every citizen as if it was their personal lapse. But whenever it came, it was enchanting. The mercury went down and did not rise for another six months. The monsoon merged imperceptibly into a mild winter. Men put on their light tropical suits and women took out their silks and shawls for the evenings.

Broad cement-concrete roads; neat, clean streets, single-storeyed houses, numerous archaeological monuments and the lush greenery were simply enchanting.

The demographic profile of Hyderabad was unusual. A Muslim Nizam ruled over a population which was preponderantly

Hindu—over eighty-seven per cent. Its medium of instruction and administration was Urdu while the mother tongues of the majority were Telugu, Marathi and Kannada in the same order. Men, irrespective of their religion, wore the dress identified with Muslims in the rest of India. Similarly, women of all faiths wore saris. Everyone spoke Urdu with an overlay of Dakhni. In short Hyderabad was a Shangri-La with a confusing fusion. It cast a magic spell on me.

The lately 'empoored' jagirdars and the nobles of the Nizam – proud but courteous – looked for friendly souls amongst the elite of the new order. The suave civil servants of Hyderabad made warm and gracious hosts. To me the city with its people looked so much like Lahore, my lost paradise.

I did not realize at that time that politically Hyderabad had been humbled only a decade ago. The Police Action of 1948 had brought around a refractory state within the political fold of independent India. It was still in the process of transition from a feudal oligarchy into a democratic polity when the reorganization of states occurred on 1 November 1956. That abolished the identity of the state of Hyderabad. Political leaders of Telangana were against the merger while leaders of Andhra were bent upon that. Ultimately the latter prevailed and Hyderabad leaders were placated by the incorporation of a 'Gentleman's Agreement'. The people of Hyderabad in general and Muslims in particular were still in a sulk at the turn of events. In fact, most never came out of it. The sentiment congealed over time into an ulcer. There was considerable resentment amongst the local people, and particularly the civil servants, against the people of the erstwhile Andhra state. Hyderabadis generally referred to them as the 'Huns' who had 'invaded' their beautiful city. On the other hand, Andhra officials considered their Hyderabadi counterparts easygoing.

The ulcer erupted first in the form of Telangana Agitation in 1969 and as a reaction to it by Andhra officers, the Jai Andhra Movement in 1972.

The Telangana revolt resurfaced in 2001 and finally culminated in the bifurcation of the state on 2 June 2014.

*

On a personal plane, I did not comprehend at that time that within the first three decades of my life I had been a victim of one revolution – the partition of the country – and a witness to another. I also wondered whether my posting at Hyderabad was my compensation for the loss of Lahore. It was a popular saying in the Punjab that one who had not seen Lahore had not yet been born!

Coming to Hyderabad I felt twice-born.

The city of Hyderabad was founded as 'a replica of heaven' in 1591. The German architect Jean Pieper holds that it was not a figure of speech but a genuine attempt to translate the concept of Islamic heaven into an architectural metaphor.

In the popular mind it is associated with the love story of Sultan Mohammad Quli Qutb Shah (1580-1611) and a dancer and singer, Bhagmati. He named the city Bhagnagar after his beloved, Bhagmati.

Later, it was nurtured as the capital of a feudal state for over two centuries. After it became capital of the enlarged state of Andhra Pradesh in 1956, it fell victim to a rapid, haphazard growth. A sudden swell in population and the push for industrial development resulted in a construction boom. The lack of matching urban planning led to a growing deterioration in civic amenities. Broad footpaths were swallowed up by widened roads, trees were felled recklessly to raise new buildings, a number of green patches were destroyed, and lakes – a distinguishing feature of the Deccan – were encroached and built upon during the dry season. Another geophysical feature,

2.5 billion-year-old rocks were blasted to make way for buildings. Low houses gave way to multi-storeyed complexes and then to malls. All these made the city congested – and warmer.

Nawab and his Car

In 1956 as IAS trainees in the districts, we used to come to Hyderabad for departmental examinations. We stayed in the 'Bella Vista', the palace of the former Prince of Berar which became the property of the government and was turned into a state guesthouse. Embossed crockery, silver cutlery and extremely polite staff gave us the feel of the fabled past just gone by. It later came to house the Administrative Staff College of India.

Once we stayed with one of Bindi's cousins who was a major in the army and posted at Hyderabad. He was a tenant of an ex-nawab living at Masab Tank. A derelict car lay jacked up in his compound. One day I noticed that the nawab went out in a rickshaw and came back with a battery and four tyres. After fitting his old car with these, he had a bath, put on a sherwani and drove out with his begum for a dinner in style. On returning, he repeated the drill in the reverse order and reverted to his Cinderella status.

Stately mansions and public buildings dotted the city. '*Lakdi ka pull*' was still true to its name – a wooden foot bridge over the railway track. The road going past Raj Bhavan was a narrow ribbon wide enough for just single lane traffic. Panjagutta was one wide open area with five rock outcrops which gave it the name. It was dominated by 'Iram Manzil', the palace of Nawab Fakhrul Mulk, a noble ranking next only to the Paigahs. It had 600 rooms and a whole host of facilities including two full-sized polo grounds. It was acquired by the government and was allotted to the public works department. The employees soon transformed the palatial building into a typical office building scrawling graffiti on the plastered walls. At its feet on the left a residential colony was built for the lower secretariat staff. None from the newcomers could imagine the past glory of the palace and its environs. The Bashir Bagh Palace, property of one of the three Paigah families, was converted into the office of the director of printing – and then was demolished. There was something melancholy about the way in which edifices of the old order were crumbling one by one, bit by bit.

There was only one shop near the Panjagutta crossroads. It was called 'Mohsin Ali Mulla Fida Ali and Sons' – an incipient supermarket selling petrol and groceries. That friendly shop has long disappeared. New-generation giant shopping malls were to sprout later everywhere gobbling up empty spaces and demolishing private residences.

In the shadow of the Naubat Pahad and between Public Gardens and the Nizam College was the vast stretch of open land called Fateh Maidan – Victory Square. It was so called because the victorious army of Emperor Aurangzeb had camped there during the siege of the Golkonda Fort in 1687. It was used for sports, parades and large public meetings. In 1967 some sports enthusiasts convinced the chief minister, Brahamananda Reddy, to build a sports stadium there. That was the beginning of the end of open spaces in the city.

In Hyderabad there was only one decent – 'modern' by the standards of the sixties to eighties – shopping centre. Though it was a big bazaar, it was called 'Abid Shop' after the first shop which was set up by a former valet of the Sixth Nizam, an Armenian Christian named Albert Abid. The airport was a small building on the other side of Begumpet which name it carried. It was built on a piece of land given to the sister of the Sixth Nizam for her *Paan ka kharcha* – expenses on Paan. There was no security check at the airport. One walked into the tarmac and got into a waiting Dakota.

The Great Flood

Hyderabad had been devastated by the worst flood in history in 1908. A third of the city was destroyed and 15,000 persons were killed. After that a reconstruction plan was prepared by the famed engineer Visveswarayya. New, broad cement concrete roads were laid and new public buildings were constructed. The city looked beautiful and justifiably earned the sobriquet of a 'bride amongst cities' of India. I fell in love with it on first sight – and the 'affair' continued.

Because of my job, I was a part of the reception team for dignitaries like the president and prime minister, besides foreign leaders. I saw the last Nizam whenever he came to receive the president or the prime minister.

Dinner in a Pantry

Cocktails and dinner parties used to be aplenty. When you were invited to a party, you noted the date, not the time. The first time, as a novice, I arrived at a dinner punctually at the Malwala Palace at eight pm. A servant told us casually that '*Saab paani nahaa rahe hain.*' It meant that our host was taking 'bath with water' – a habit peculiar to Hyderabadis. I asked the servant if I was at the right place. He replied that there was going to be a dinner, not evening tea! The host emerged after a good half hour wringing his hands in a gesture of apology for the delay. It was an hour before the first guest ambled in. Drinking started and the party started warming gradually. Around eleven, famished as a teetotaller, I first dropped hints and then begged for dinner. The host said guests were still coming.

And he had to wait. When I appealed again after some time, he said that he could have us served in the pantry provided we sneaked out unnoticed. Since then we have grown wiser. We go to most parties at least two hours after the given time and still are one of the earliest. In Hyderabad it is a good policy to eat your dinner at home and then go for dinner.

The *Deccan Chronicle* founded in 1938 was the only English paper apart from a remote second – *The Daily News* – which subsequently closed down. The proprietor-editor-publisher brothers – Nandgopal and Pattabhiram – were genial Mudaliars and we often met socially. The paper gave all sorts of news – even of the death of persons who we didn't know had ever lived. However, no controversies or scandals were ever reported. In 1977 it was purchased by a civil contractor from Andhra. Subsequent editors became anonymous. Later, some new papers like the *Newstime* and the *A.P. Times* also emerged, as did some in Telugu and Urdu. *Eenadu*, a Telugu daily, broke new ground by publishing simultaneous multiple editions and claimed the largest circulation of any Telugu daily. Much later, *The Hindu, The Indian Express* and *The Times of India* started their regional editions from Hyderabad.

The Ritz in Hyderabad and the Percy's Hotel in Secunderabad were the only Western hotels. The latter was next to the Plaza Cinema. It had a bar attached to it and one could pick up a glass of beer from that and watch the movie in style. A cinema house we often visited for English movies was the Embassy which was so small and quaint that it gave us the illusion of a private theatre. All of them were pulled down later to make way for large commercial properties. The tall Taj Mahal hotel used to serve a 'special thali' of Udipi meals in family cabins at the fabulous price of Rs 2 per head. It was later dwarfed by taller structures.

The *Siasat* started in 1949 was the leading Urdu daily. Both its co-founders, Abid Ali Khan and Mehboob Husain Jigar, were respected figures in the city. I met most Urdu men of letters in Khan's house. I also met people from various cultural, linguistic and regional groups at other places. It was a captivating mosaic. Syed Hashim Ali, a civil servant of Hyderabad, introduced me to the subtle kinship of a lifelong friendship. I met many more remarkable persons but none left as good a mark on me as Syed Hashim Ali and Abid Ali Khan – and later Abid Husain and Air Chief Marshall Idris Latif and his charming wife, Bilquis.

The city used to have trailer-buses and had the largest number of bicycles in the country. The Salar Jung Museum located in its quaint original setting, the Dewan Deodi, hereditary residence of the Salar Jung family, had a mystique about it which disappeared when it was shifted to a new type-design government building.

At evening parties, the poems of the Junior Prince, Moazzam Jah, who sported the pen name of Shajih, were recited by professional and amateur singers – and relished by guests. Now one hears them rarely. Jamila Bano and Vithal Rao used to enthral the audience with their rendition of ghazals. I met and made friends with Makhdoom Mohiuddin, the legendary poet, and his friend Dr Raj Bahadur Gour, both Communist leaders. It was a rare treat to hear Makhdoom recite his own poems at a party at Abid's house. The rotund and ever-smiling Aziz Warsi was reputed to be the best *qawwali* singer in the country.

Balamurlikrishna was singing his way to the pinnacle of Carnatic music and the young Yamini Krishnamurthy used to be specially invited from Chennai for the performance at official functions of Andhra's own classical dance form – Kuchipudi. The lucid, verbal interpretation of her father in English added to the magic of her captivating performance. For some reason, there was no tradition of theatre in Hyderabad.

Mystique of the Old City

Parts of the old city evoked descriptions of the streets of Damascus of Arabian Nights.

A fascinating vista opened up as one crossed the Naya Pul on the Musi river into the old city. Irani cafes sold not coffee but tea. They must have been the first fast food joints in the world. They were popular with budding poets who, after ordering a cup of tea, would proceed to inflict their latest poem on some hapless customer.

Apart from the Irani chai, some other types of tea were also sold in the city.

Kaddak chai was tea brewed over and over again till it became dark brown – and bitter. The colour and taste were moderated by adding sugar and a dash of milk.

Khada chamcha (literally, standing spoon) was a variety of tea which was made so thick with sugar that a spoon could stand erect in the cup. Diabetes originated with that practice.

Ghade wali chai was unique inasmuch as it was boiled over slow fire in a large earthen pot. It had an earthy flavour as with tea served in *kullar*s – earthen cups – in some railway trains in the north.

Kanjaal daar chai was tea with milk cream beaten into flakes covering the top like moss covers stagnant waters (kanjaal means moss).

Burqa wali chai was tea with cream covering the decoction and spilling over from the glass tumbler. It was given with an opium pill and was sold in one shop which had a license to sell opium.[6]

---

[6] For the finer points about the varieties of tea, I am indebted to my friend B.N. Raman

Chocolate tea remains popular even now and is sold by Lasa and Lamsa.

*

There was an old person known as Siddi[7] Baba, reputed for his crystal gazing. Once there was a minor theft in our house. My daughter, Sandhya, went to him for help and also to test his claims. He poured some water on a ceramic plate and invited any pre-pubescent girl or boy to see the view. The image seen floating on still water on the plate was that of a kleptomaniac friend of the children.

There was an Arab group who, after singing and dancing themselves into a trance, pierced their bodies with spikes without spilling a drop of blood. Some of their members walked barefoot on burning coal. I organized their performances as a part of the tourist attractions of the city. They were grateful for the financial help they thus received.

*

Urdu language ruled the city and its streets were littered with poets. The city justly acquired international reputation for its *mushaira*s. Thousands of people paid to listen to Urdu poets recite their poems in large open grounds till well past midnight.

Hyderabad became a haven for Urdu poets and writers after the north Indian courts of Lucknow and Rampur ceased to exist in the nineteenth century. The *ghazal* – the lyrical genre of Urdu poetry – was, and remains, the most popular. Each couplet of a ghazal is a unit by itself. In its concision and depth, I believe only the Japanese Haiku poem surpasses it. Its recitation greeted with vociferous and repeated bouts of praise is equivalent to an encore. The poet who

[7] Siddi is a generic term for migrants from Abyssinia

wins the most approbation is much like the 'man of the match' in today's cricket. In Urdu he is credited with having 'looted' the mushaira.

Attending a mushaira is a unique experience. It has a traditional setting, a ceremonial and a participative mystique not found in any other language. Some good poets like the late Suleiman Khateeb could bring tears to the eyes of the audience.

Alas, the tradition has all but disappeared today.

Jokes by and on Jamaluddin, the legendary superintendent of Public Gardens, enlivened most gatherings. The old gentry were truly laid back. The famed cosmopolitan culture of Hyderabad was slowly unfolding before me and wrapping me in its warm embrace.

***

England, Europe, West Asia and Back

In early 1964 I was selected as a British Council scholar for a postgraduate course in Industrial Management at the Leeds University. The Council booked my passage by sea. It was a new experience and I enjoyed a twenty-one-day paid holiday.

At that time rules about travelling abroad were very rigid and so it was difficult for Bindi to go with me. However, she joined me after three months and, being a trained teacher, got a job immediately.

We left our two children, Rahul, aged seven, and Sandhya, around five, with my parents in Gurgaon. Both my parents and the children enjoyed the arrangement. Grandparents had the full-time charge of the kids and the children had the full attention of the doting old couple. Gurgaon then was a sleepy small town. Both children recall that period as the best in their early life.

England was short of teachers, physicians, surgeons, nurses, bus drivers and conductors. The entire social service sector was serviced by Indians and Pakistanis. That was because of the loss of about half a million young men and women in the Second World War. The demographic damage inflicted by wars has a long-term impact. It hit Britain's economy and damaged its social fabric. It was widely believed that if the Indians withdrew from England, their social services would collapse.

Before Bindi's arrival, while looking for accommodation, I saw an ad in one of the windows of a shop near the university by a professor asking for help in exchange for free accommodation. Bindi was required to iron their clothes twice a week and clean the house with a vacuum cleaner once a week. In exchange, we got the attic flat with a kitchen and the use of the bathroom. The lady of the house, Pat, had been a nurse and so she was overawed by Bindi when she got a teacher's job. Since Bindi was on probation, I helped her and we did a thorough job of vacuum-cleaning the house. Pat advised Bindi to iron only collars of shirts since they were their only visible parts. Pat would set up the ironing board for Bindi, bring her some tea, help her sort out the clothes and chat with her while she did the work. In exchange, she would do our laundry whenever she used her washing machine.

With Bindi's arrival we suddenly felt very rich. With free lodging, we could easily live within my scholarship of £57-10 per month. Bindi's salary of £100 a month was left for us to blow up any way we liked.

The British Council used to organize tours of different duration – for weekends, for a week and a fortnight. We made use of those and saw a lot of places in England.

It was good to experience university life in England. It was a cultural shock for me to see how some students sat in the class with their feet up on the low table in front of them and address the lecturers by their first names. Also they often challenged their statements and argued them out. The students' union managed all aspects of life in the university except teaching.

Bindi earned her certification of a qualified and permanent teacher in England and the Commonwealth.

In Israel

I returned to India by a hopping flight which gave me stopovers at Paris, Rome, Frankfurt Athens, Istanbul, Cairo, Tel Aviv and finally Tehran.

At that time India did not recognize Israel diplomatically since it was a theocratic state. No Muslim country in West Asia allowed any passenger with a passport carrying an Israeli visa into its territory. Our high commission in London therefore issued me another passport for use exclusively for my visit to Israel. The old passport was to be used for visits to other Muslim countries around it.

I spent a week in Israel as a guest of Moshe, a Jew I had befriended in England. Every morning Moshe drove me to different cities and tourist places. On the fourth day, when I asked him where we would be going that day, he said, 'You have seen the whole country. I will take you to some of my friends in a new settlement.'

I was impressed by the transformation by the Jews of a desert into blooming greenery.

*

In Hyderabad, chief secretary Anatharaman showed invidious discrimination in his behaviour towards me. While one of my colleagues was granted study leave for an identical scholarship, I was granted earned leave. The difference was that while my colleague got half his salary for the period of study, I had to forego that benefit. Anatharaman turned down my plea for fair play. On appeal, the chief minister, Brahamananda Reddy, overruled him and upheld my plea.

*

There are numerous comical instances relating to Anatharaman, but I will mention just two.

He used green ink in his pen while I used black ink for noting in the files. One day he minuted 'Pl spk.' on a file that I had submitted to him. It is generally used when the superior officer wants elucidation on some point. I got mentally prepared for a grilling. When I entered his room, he looked at me and after a pause, asked me, 'I say, what ink do you use?'

Surprised, I told him it was black.

'Where do you get it?'

I was relieved that it had nothing to do with my noting on the file, only with my ink. The Parker pen company used to make inks earlier, but at that time, the import was banned. An Indian company called 'Quink' had started manufacturing it in the country lately. I said it was available in all good stationery shops in the market.

'Why do you use black?'

I said, 'Sir, that is the original colour which has been used right from the beginning in all official documents.'

'Is it very costly?'

'No, Sir, if you like, I'll ask your PA to get it for you.'

'No, no,' he whispered in a conspiratorial tone, as he always did when he wanted to give some serious advice, 'I would like to buy it on my private account.'

I got worried. The implication of his remark was that I was guilty of official malpractice in indenting it from the department. But the entire set of stationery was always supplied by the office everywhere, I reassured myself. To him I said, 'In that case, I will get it purchased on your private account.'

Those who had to put up with his eccentricities may like to note who was behind the historic change of colour of Anatharaman's notes and minutes from green to black.

Once the American ambassador, Galbraith, was coming to inaugurate a US-funded project in Medak about forty-five kilometres from Hyderabad. I received sudden summons from Anatharaman that morning.

I felt at ease when he asked me, 'What sort of dress do you think I should wear for the function?' After all, the dispenser of any advice is conceded a superior status, however momentary.

'Sir, he is going to be in his bush shirt. So, you can also be easy.' I had seen Galbraith earlier in Nagarjunasagar not only in such a dress but also snatching a head load of mortar from a labourer and carrying it on his head all the way up the scaffolding.

'No, no,' he whispered, 'He may do anything, but I am the chief secretary. I must observe protocol.' I saw his point and changed my tack, 'In that case, Sir, a lounge suit will do.'

'Why not a buttoned-up suit? I have a number of them.'

I said that would be fine too.

'But I have a collection of lounge suits too. What colour?'

I did not want to suggest any colour or shade. Suppose he did not have that? I said any colour would do.

He was not satisfied. He said, 'I say, you come with me. My house is on the way in Secunderabad. I will show you my suits. We will decide then.'

He took me inside his bedroom, flung open his wardrobe and showed me his collection. Certainly he had far more suits than I had. 'And all imported wool,' he said. He took them out one by one, described when and where the cloth was bought, and where each suit was stitched.

Finally, he chose a cream-coloured buttoned-up suit. I was relieved that no selection of tie would be involved. After he had dressed up, he came out into the drawing room where I was waiting. Looking at him I said he was looking fabulous. A servant brought two cups of steaming, home-made coffee. I greatly enjoyed the delicious coffee. The best coffee can be made only in south Indian homes.

During the two-hour journey to the site, he downloaded half an encyclopedia of good administrative practices onto my empty head. The other half was done on the drive back to the city.

***

A Spell in Delhi

After a few weeks I was posted as deputy secretary in the ministry of mines and metals headed by the legendary S.K. Dey as the minister.

Dey had resigned from an American multinational selling air-conditioners in India and sought an appointment with the prime minister. When it was not granted, he would go every morning and sit at the gate of the Teen Murti House, the official residence of Prime Minister Jawaharlal Nehru. After forty days of seeing Dey as a regular fixture every morning and evening, Nehru finally sent for him and asked him what he wanted. Dey was a highly persuasive salesman. He sold the concept of community development to Nehru. As a result of that, he was appointed as administrator of the first community development project in Nilokheri in the present-day Haryana. My batch of IAS officers had spent a week doing '*shram dan*' – physical labour for building a road at Nilokheri. Later the scheme was introduced all over India, the department upgraded to a ministry, and Dey appointed as minister of community development. After Nehru's death, Indira Gandhi transferred him from community development and posted him as minister of mines and metals.

I had to work under a joint secretary named R.N. Vasudeva. From day one we did not hit it off with each other. He found fault with me about everything. When the situation became unbearable, and the relations became impossible, Dey put me through his own test to form a judgement about me. First, he asked me to handle the arrangements for the national conference of mining ministers and when it was over at five-thirty pm he said that he wanted the draft minutes of the conference before he went to bed. I was able to meet his deadline.

Then he took me on a week-long tour of the northeast. Immediately on return, I had to prepare an exhaustive draft of his tour notes. I scraped through that ordeal too. The only fault he found with me was that I did not eat as well as he did and should eat more. He was a gourmet and knew where a culinary specialty could be found in any corner of India. Once he made his party take a detour of sixty kilometres from the highway just to pick up a special dish from a remote town of Assam. He was blessed with an enormous appetite. I saw him eat a full chicken immediately after breakfast on his tour. He used to boast that it was the chickens' energy that kept him charged both in his words as well as in his work.

On return to Delhi, he ordered that I should be placed under another joint secretary. My life became normal.

In the elections of 1967, Indira Gandhi did not give him any ticket. He went into oblivion after that.

After the elections Indira Gandhi upgraded the ministry by adding the department of steel & heavy engineering to it. Dr M. Channa Reddy from Andhra Pradesh was appointed to it as a cabinet minister. He took me on as his special assistant and the whole world changed for me.

Budha Goraya today. Photo courtesy: Sayed Babar Ali

The canal 'Aik' which gave my ancestor the nickname 'Ludher'. Photo courtesy: Sayed Babar Ali

Left: My paternal grandfather Kirpa Ram
Right: Maternal grandfather Kripa Sagar

Left: My father Mela Ram, 1898-1972
Right: My mother Lila Vati, 1903-1989

A typical refugee train. We travelled in one such from Rawalpindi to Amritsar, 18-21 October 1947

Greeting Prime Minister Nehru at the Begumpet airport, Hyderabad, 1959

Rahul and Sandhya at a party, 1962

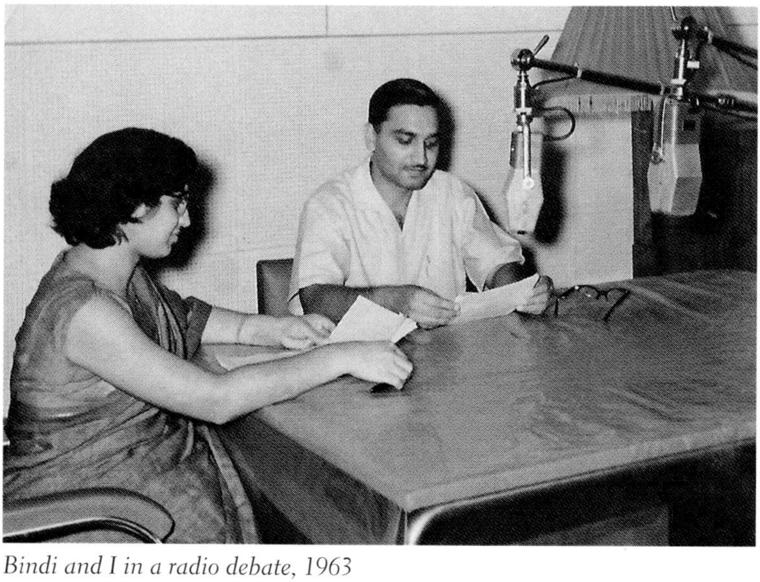

Bindi and I in a radio debate, 1963

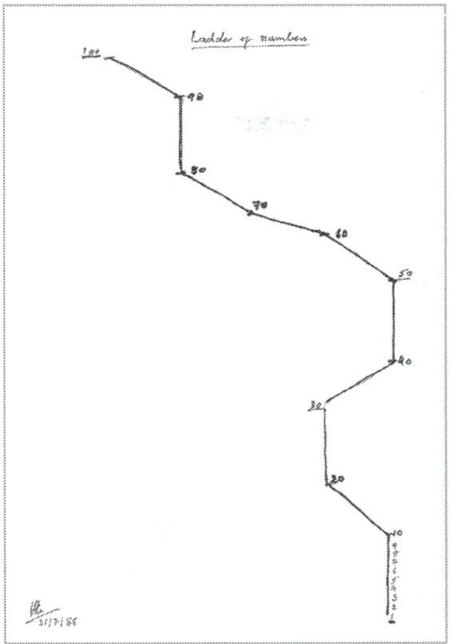

Left: How I visualize numerals 1-100
Right: Brilliant insight. My favourite cartoon by Turhan Selcuk.
Photo courtesy: Director 'The House of Humour & Satire', Gabrovo, Bulgaria 1985

Reading my composition at a reception at Lahore in 2005

Family portrait in 2009. Seated: Bindi and self, with grandson Rishabh on my left. Standing: (left to right) granddaughter Raisa, daughter Sandhya, daughter-in-law Rajeshwari, son Rahul

Rahul and Ayesha in the play written by him, 1975

Granddaughter Raisa - psychotherapist and Bharatanatyam dancer

Bindi and I in front of my maternal grandfather's house in Lahore under demolition for 'development' in 2005

Bindi with the granddaughter of the maid of her grandmother in front of Bindi's ancestral house in Bhalwal in 2005. A high school was running in the ground floor of the three-storey house

'The Skull Rock': Rightly worried for the future of our 2,500-million-year-old rock heritage because of its reckless destruction. Photo courtesy: Anand Madabhushi

I have not seen any minister who was so sharp mentally and so well organized in his work. Whatever he wanted done, he would note down in his notebook. Identical notebooks were given to me and the personal assistants and the contents of his diary distributed amongst us according to our designated jobs.

He wanted daily reports on the progress of action on each item. If the item was not disposed of, it was carried over to the next day. It was scored off only after action had been taken one way or the other.

Dr Channa Reddy was good at picking experts' brains. He had a library of brief notes given to him by experts from various fields. That constituted his bedside reading.

One day he returned fuming from a meeting with the deputy chairman of the Planning Commission for which the secretary, N.C. Srivastava, and Vasudeva had accompanied him. He threw the file on the desk and said in disgust, 'What do you do when the secretary does not speak and the joint secretary does not know!'

He therefore did not agree to Vasudeva's extension despite a letter of recommendation from Nijlingappa who was then the president of the ruling Congress party. I felt a perverse satisfaction at Vasudeva's comeuppance.

*

In April 1968 the supreme court delivered its judgment in the election petition against Channa Reddy holding him guilty of malpractice in elections and disqualified him for any electoral office for six years.

He had a tremendous temper and lost it liberally in direct proportion to the seniority of the recipient of his ire. That earned him the enmity of many influential persons in Delhi.

After Channa Reddy's departure, the steel department took me in and placed me under a joint secretary called Sabanayagam. He had a large and golden heart that gave more than full credit to the work done by officers under him.

Once he asked me to draft a speech for the minister's use for an intervention in the debate for grants for the ministry. Sabanayagam went through it, signed it and sent it up. Later, the minister K.C. Pant complimented him for a very good draft in the presence of the secretary R.C. Dutt. Sabanayagam told him that draft was not his but mine. Back in his room, he called me to pass on the minister's compliment to me. I felt amazed because it was for the first time that in Delhi I saw a boss let an opportunity pass by to grab credit at the expense of his deputies.

For some time Swaran Singh was the cabinet minister of steel in addition to his regular charge of another ministry. I was handling the Bhilai Steel Plant which was built with the technical and financial assistance of Soviet Russia. Once the Soviet minister for foreign economic aid, Kuznetsov, came to India and visited Bhilai. He was very critical of some delays. He pulled up the general manager of the plant in front of his staff and workers. Gesticulating crudely, he put his hand in his pocket and said that Soviet money was not for wasting.

Later in the evening, Swaran Singh threw a large party for Kuznetsov. Drinking went on till midnight. Swaran Singh, a teetotaller, sat quietly in a chair while his chief guest and others downed vodka. Some of us who did not drink sat listening to Swaran Singh. Recalling the incident mentioned above, Singh said, 'See how shabbily the donors of aid treat their clients!'

Galbraith's Inspiration

After serving my tenure and missing my promotion, I returned to Hyderabad in September 1970.

At the railway book stall at Wardha I picked up a copy of *The New Industrial State* by the renowned American economist J.K. Galbraith. I quote below an extract from it to illustrate its sheer beauty and insight:

> ...Clearly some individuals do add luster to organization. The accomplishments of the great physician are his own, not those of the hospital where he serves. The achievements of the poet are his own, not those of the institution where he is currently the artist in residence. Similarly, the opera singer or actor and, though not always, the great scientist.
>
> Men are, in fact, either sustained by organization or sustain organization. They are either esteemed because of organization or the organization is esteemed because of them. The individual is himself rarely a sound judge of these matters. Those who are esteemed because of organization almost invariably attribute the acclaim to their own personality.
>
> But there is an infallible test. That is to observe what happens to the individual when he leaves the organization or retires. The great physician is not greatly diminished by being separated from his hospital. Nor, except as regards regular salary, is the poet when he leaves the university. Nor is the competent newspaperman when he moves on. Nor the great scientist nor the entertainer. They sustained, were not sustained by, the organization to which they belonged...[8]

I resolved at that time that I will endeavour to belong to the second type of persons. I *will have* a life after retirement – independent of any organizational crutches.

In Hyderabad I was appointed director of industries. Because of that position, I became chairman/director of the board of about twenty companies.

---

[8] J.K. Galbraith, *The New Industrial State* (New York: Signet Paperback, 1968), p. 107

Bindi, who had continued her teaching after our return from England, got a job in the Hyderabad Public School and later in the Administrative Staff College of India as a Research Associate. My son Rahul was admitted in the Hyderabad Public School and daughter, Sandhya, to the St. Ann's High School.

A 'Mother-in-law'

Everything seemed to have fallen into place perfectly – that is everything but one. My boss, the secretary of the industries department, was Anil De. He had been director of industries some years earlier. Our relationship therefore turned out to be a typical case of mother-in-law and daughter-in-law. He had invented the wheel and therefore believed that there was no further scope for any change or improvement. For everything, he said, he had left a file in the directorate which I needed to locate to find guidance and enlightenment.

There were two additional directors in the department. He made them independent but held me responsible for their drafts of minutes of meetings, etc. They also nurtured their own cliques and had his ear.

De was a finicky person who spent a lot of time on style rather than the substance of the matter. He had a turn of phrase which he showed in his demi-official letters. Once he spent the better part of a day approving a draft of an invitation card for the function for laying the foundation stone for the Visakhapatnam Steel Plant by Prime Minister Indira Gandhi. For any project report prepared by us, he scrutinized the design of the cover page but ignored the content. He avoided meetings where he had to face his superior or peers to argue his case.

Once he called me at noon to say that he had accepted an invitation to address the National Association of Steel Re-rollers at the Ritz Hotel at five pm. Due to an important and unforeseen development, he would not be able to go there. I should therefore deputize for him. I mumbled feebly that the notice was too short and the Association might not like me to stand in for him. He flattered me by saying that it should be no problem for someone like me. I spent the afternoon preparing myself for the meeting. While I was addressing the meeting, I suddenly noticed a spitting image of De sitting on the far side of the first row. After I had finished my address, I walked up to the man to tell him how much he resembled my boss. As I got near him, I found that he was, in fact, De himself. Before I could ask him anything, he smiled and said, 'Well done, old boy,' and joined the audience for tea.

Gaddafi's Libya

In 1972 I was sent by the government of India as adviser on small-scale industries to Libya for three months. There I had the experience of living in a police state. The Libyan government put me up in a hotel on the beach of the Mediterranean Sea. There was another Indian and some Egyptian experts also staying in the same hotel. Besides free board and lodging, we were paid five Libyan pounds a day by way of out-of-pocket allowance. The assignment therefore wasn't attractive in monetary terms. The capital, Tripoli, was a small, neat but dull place with nothing by way of diversion. The local TV telecast news and trials of political prisoners under the new revolutionary dictatorship of Col. Gaddafi.

The local officers were lazy and incompetent. Once the head of the ministry asked me to visit a sick confectionery company and suggest how it could be restored to health. I asked the managing director some basic questions about capital investment, working capital, loan, etc. Before I returned to the secretariat, a complaint had been made to the secretary that I was asking for 'secret' information. I was very angry at this attitude and asked the secretary how I could suggest anything without getting basic information. He smiled and asked me not to bother. I completed my report in two months and suggested, inter alia, the establishment of a corporation. The minister promptly issued orders and said that I would be its first chairman. I got alarmed and said I was not interested. Taleyar Khan, the Indian ambassador, tried to pressurize me but I stuck to my decision.

While settling my account, the Libyans deducted income tax and Jihad tax against Israel from my meagre out-of-pocket allowance. I protested that my allowance was not taxable and that I was not their citizen and so was not subject to Jihad tax. They had a high level meeting about it and, after discussing it for half a day, overruled my objection.

I was glad to escape alive from such a prison. On the way I spent a week in Beirut with a friend. It was a lovely place at that time before it got embroiled in deadly conflicts and civil war.

*

Back in Hyderabad, I created two corporations which were the first in the country. One was the leather development corporation and the other was the industrial infrastructure corporation. I would like to mention an interesting incident relating to the second corporation.

The industries department had a budget head for 'industrial estates and industrial areas'. Through that the department used to acquire land, develop it and allot it at fixed rates to prospective entrepreneurs looking for land to set up medium and large industrial units. It was a fixed amount and lapsed if it was not utilized within the financial year. I proposed the creation of the industrial infrastructure corporation. If the amount budgeted for industrial areas was routed through that corporation, we could raise additional funds from banks and increase the availability of the amount by 250 per cent. Further, the amount would not lapse at the end of the financial year.

CAG's pat

During the annual statutory audit of the department by the comptroller and auditor general (CAG), the team generally raises audit objections which have to be answered by the head of the department. If the objections are not met satisfactorily, they are included in the CAG's audit report to the legislature. The public accounts committee then examines them and top officers have to submit explanations personally. It is a situation which all officers wish to avoid. The audit report is therefore rightly dreaded, as the country saw in the case of the coal scam under the last UPA government at the Centre.

At the end of his audit, the leader of the audit team asked to see me personally. I wondered what objection he was going to highlight to me. To my pleasant surprise, he said, 'Generally we are known as fault-finders. But today I want to tell you that we are recording our appreciation of the initiative taken by you for the creation of the infrastructure corporation and will recommend its replication.' Such an out-of-the-way laudatory remark is most unusual.

I brought this to De's notice through a demi-official letter. Sometime after that, I was shocked at getting a letter from the chief secretary conveying the adverse remarks made by Anil De in my annual confidential report. It said about me: 'An intelligent and hardworking officer, but needs to develop in view of the expanding responsibilities of the department.' I felt deeply hurt – and amused. Is there any human being who does not need to develop? And expanding responsibilities were created by me.

The remark was expunged when I challenged it. Anil De himself earned a severe adverse report from the chief secretary. He cried on my shoulder and I could not bring myself to ask him about what he had done to me.

*

Before my promotion to super-time scale, I was appointed as collector of Hyderabad.

There is little revenue work in the capital district. The commissioner of police handles law and order. And there are too many VIPs to snatch the limelight from the collector. However, Hyderabad had not yet been divided into two districts.

I spent four months in that job.

* * *

The Bottled Devil

Both my son, Rahul, and daughter, Sandhya, were very good in studies.

Rahul started the monthly magazine of the school 'Shaheen' and became quite well known for that. He wrote a very beautiful poetic play in English about the renunciation of Gautama Buddha (published by Partridge in 2015). He also played the lead role in it. That won him a lot of praise from his friends and the elite of the city. That sort of early fame seemed to have gone to his head.

*

I think he was initiated into drinking in the final year of high school. There were plenty of students who were sons of rich businessmen with lots of money to throw about in the school.

However, Rahul passed his Senior Cambridge with a very high score and got a gold medal in English. At that time, the reputation of Osmania University was tarnished by frequent strikes and agitations. We therefore sent him to Delhi. Since no hostel accommodation was available, he took a sharing accommodation with two other students. On one of my visits to Delhi, I went to look him up and was appalled to notice the absence of any academic ambience in his lodging. Rahul got into drug abuse there.

After his graduation in 1976, Rahul shocked us by refusing to study further whereas we had planned to send him to the US for higher studies.

He got a job in a reputed company where his starting salary was more than mine in the super-time scale of IAS. However, he did not make any gesture of contributing towards household expenses. On the other hand, he used to run up a high bill on my account in the Secunderabad Club. I warned him many times that it was beyond my capacity to pay such steep bills. It had no effect on him. Fed up, I had him barred from the club.

Being a teetotaller family, we were blissfully ignorant about the nature of drug addiction and its treatment. We believed that drinking was a problem of lapse from good character and that some sane advice or serious warning would put him back on the track. It was of no avail. Gradually, he became withdrawn from us. He went out whenever he liked, came home late and slipped into his room quietly. He would ask the maid for whatever he needed. The maid's husband had died of drinking at a young age. She therefore knew how to handle a person given to drinking.

Being irregular in his attendance, Rahul lost his job. Thereafter a regular pattern emerged. He kept on getting good jobs and also losing them with equal rapidity.

Finally, a time came when he was always drunk. His behaviour with us also became very rude. He started questioning our judgement, our wisdom, and even our sanity.

The top psychiatrist in the government gave us a liquid to mix in Rahul's drink. That, he said, would produce revulsion in Rahul against alcohol. We tried that but it had no effect on Rahul. He rebuked the maid for 'adulterating' his drink. We sent him to another leading psychiatrist. He went for some sessions and then stopped, saying that the psychiatrist did not know anything. Short of going to godmen, we tried everything but nothing worked. Rahul vehemently denied that he was an alcoholic. Just to prove his point he would go off drinks for two or three weeks. However, his heavy eyes betrayed him. Obviously he was taking some drug – or sleeping pills.

Sandhya Neglected

All this time our daughter, Sandhya, suffered the unintended and unconscious neglect of the emotional needs of a young growing girl since our entire attention was focused on Rahul. Her school was reputed to be the best school for girls. However, she did not have happy memories of those years. Its rows of cellular grey rooms, high walls and windows with steel bars lent it a penitentiary air. Like most Indian schools it discouraged originality. At my request, she was exempted from the Bible studies period and sent to the library for that duration. That inculcated in her a life-long love for books.

She scored a very high rank in Senior Cambridge. Thereafter she wanted to study geography and art for her degree course. However, after our experience with Rahul, we did not let her go to the Delhi University. She had perforce to join the local Nizam College. The uninspiring department of geography at that college completely squashed her interest in that subject.

One day, she surprised all of us by getting a fellowship for post-graduation in International Relations at the European centre of the Johns Hopkins University at Bologna in Italy. She had applied without our knowledge.

Sandhya spent two years in Italy. She started attending yoga classes which she practised with zeal for over ten years.

On return, she worked as the coordinator of a women's international film festival and organized events in Delhi, Mumbai and Chennai for about a year. We recalled her to Hyderabad when there was a job offer for her. Somehow that did not work out and she felt she was tricked out of her job and stay in Delhi.

In Hyderabad she became a correspondent with an English daily called *Newstime*. She enjoyed the work and wrote some very satisfying human interest stories. She also got an attractive offer from UNI. On my advice, she gave up journalism.

Later she won a scholarship for an advanced course in German in Berlin.

On return, due to our opposition to her going to Delhi or Mumbai, Sandhya established a design and print studio at home named 'Creative Point'. To our pleasant surprise, it became a success very soon and she started making enough money to pay for a car. I got an allotment of the new Maruti car and she repaid me in monthly instalments. She ran her business very successfully for almost four years. Looking back, I feel that we did not adequately acknowledge her successes achieved entirely on her own.

Her unconscious compulsion to share our concern about Rahul prevented her from sharing her own problems and aspirations with us lest they should add to our load of worries. Her persona and dreams became almost invisible to us. She felt like a non-person. She was sick and exhausted with our obsession with Rahul. Many years later, when she voiced that grouse, we realized how right she was.

In 1989, she broke loose from her life in the shadows and accepted a good job with a publishing firm in Delhi. By nature, she inspires love and regard in every person she meets. She soon developed a circle of interesting friends from diverse fields. She began flowering as a person in her own right.

City Father

In 1974 I was promoted and posted as special officer of the Municipal Corporation of Hyderabad. This job is created when the elected body of municipal corporation is superseded and all the functions of the various elected organs of the corporation, including the ceremonial mayoral functions, are concentrated into the hands of one officer. I thus became the sole city father. The corporation was notorious for its corruption.

The first case I had to deal with arose within a few days. A builder had got permission for constructing four floors for an apartment block but proceeded to build six. On being given a notice to stop, he obtained an injunction from the high court which curiously directed the corporation 'not to interfere in the construction made or *to be made*'. Under that protective order, the builder merrily went ahead in his violation of the building permit. The injunction was vacated after the unauthorized portion had been completed. I therefore issued orders to demolish the two floors and sent a large demolition squad to complete the job over the weekend when the courts were closed. Considerable demolition had been achieved by Monday morning when the courts opened and the builder brought a stay order.

My action caused a sensation in the city and all newspapers reported the incident on their front pages, some calling it highhanded and even brutal. The legislative assembly was in session and the matter was raised there by an MLA of the Majlis-e Ittehadul Muslimeen Party (MIM).

Vengala Rao, the chief minister, quietly got up and announced that my action was commendable. That gave me a lot of confidence and strength during the rest of my tenure.

I started the practice of touring the city every Wednesday when on the spot redress of complaints was done as far as possible. Complaints requiring inspections and inquiries were registered and reviewed every week. My *pada yatra* became so well known that every city MLA wanted to accompany me in his constituency to claim credit for having brought me there.

At that time, the city was divided into six municipal circles each under an assistant commissioner. People had to come to the headquarters specially to make their representations to me. I therefore decided to sit for half day per week in each circle. During that period, I used to make spot personal inspections.

The corporation had a large fleet of trucks for conservancy work. The diesel required for them was always overbilled. The chief medical and health officer who was in charge of the fleet busted the scam and we effected a saving of sixty per cent in the bill. Thereupon the Drivers' Union controlled by the Communist party went on strike. After some days, a top leader of the party whom I knew very well came to meet me in that connection. I told him about the economy that we had been able to effect and expected that his party would acknowledge it instead of going on a strike against it. He said, 'Mr Luther, we appreciate your good work. However, my advice is that even in good things, go slow.'

When it comes to the crunch, all politicians are alike!

*

Of the many great moments in my tenure, I mention only a few of them here.

I had drawn up a comprehensive project for the improvement of slums in the city and called it 'Habitat Hyderabad'. One of the officers of the United Nations International Children's Emergency Fund (UNICEF), Bill Cousins, was associated with our community development project. When I sounded him for financial assistance, he replied that UNICEF was concerned only with children and women. I argued that in an average family only the head was a male adult; the rest were all children and women. So, if I changed the title of the project and called it 'Project for the Amelioration of the Conditions of Children and Women in the Slums of Hyderabad', would it pass muster? He smiled and shrugged his shoulders. I repackaged the project under the new title. Imagine my surprise and delight when UNICEF sanctioned it as the first pilot project in the world. Cousins later wrote a book on that. Many social service organizations like Rotary International and Lions came forward to adopt various slums. We leveraged our deposits with branches of leading banks to provide soft loans to slum dwellers to construct their houses.

Home for Leprosy Patients

On the annual Anti-Leprosy day, I made the mandatory visit to the Leprosy Home run by the municipal corporation to distribute some clothes and other goodies to the inmates.

I was appalled by the insanitary conditions in which the patients lived. Earlier, I had visited the Sivananda Rehabilitation Home for leprosy patients at Kukatpally. It was run by the late Rani Kumudini Devi, a leading and dedicated social worker of Hyderabad. In addition to their treatment, the patients were given training and employment in soft cottage industries. She had fifty acres of land which was not fully utilized. I persuaded her to accept a merger of our Leprosy Home with her facility. In exchange, I offered to transfer the annual budget of our facility to her besides building cottages for all patient families and providing all civic amenities to the new colony.

This public-private partnership turned out to be one of my most satisfying achievements during my spell in the corporation. The scheme was run on the communist principle: 'To each according to need; from each according to capacity.'

Accordingly, all able-bodied patients were required to offload the supplies of food grains and other materials from lorries. They started demanding wages for that. I said in that case they would have to pay for their board and lodging. Their demand was instigated by a female politician to cause trouble for Kumudini Devi.

However, a result of the project was that the city was rid of leper-beggars. The new project was commended by the Union ministry of social welfare as a model scheme for the whole country.

*

Some citizens of the old city complained that garbage from their streets were not picked up by the conservancy staff of the corporation. The officials explained that the trucks were too large to enter the narrow streets. I then ordered the purchase of twenty hippo-haulers and had mini trailers attached to them. It caused a sensation when they arrived to clean up the streets which had never been cleaned before.

*

I used to receive numerous petitions, mostly from the old city, written in Urdu on postcards. I would pick up a few of them for surprise personal inspection. This I did by taking a detour on the way to the office. I never went by the normal route to the office.

One day I received a postcard complaining angrily against inaction on the part of the corporation for attending to sewer discharge in front of the complainant's house. Next day my car pulled up in front of the house and my driver knocked at the door. An old man came out and asked the driver what he wanted. Meanwhile I came out and told him that I had come in answer to his letter. He started trembling and pleaded for forgiveness for his impudence. His problem was instantly solved and the news spread like wildfire in the old city.

*

The Jam Bagh Road on the left of the Muazzam Jahi market had a concentration of fruitsellers. They encroached upon a good deal of the road and scattered their trade garbage carelessly causing serious obstruction to traffic. The corporation has the authority to regulate the disposal of trade refuse in a prescribed manner. In case of non-compliance, it can undertake it itself and recover the cost from the delinquent parties. The shopkeepers ignored the notice issued to them in that regard. We then ordered a round-the-clock employment of tractor trailers to remove all the scattered trade refuse and started sending them daily bills. The association of traders issued condemnatory statements and approached my minister and the chief minister. They were firmly sent away.

*

The next campaign was undertaken at the chief minister's instance. There was a seventy-feet wide road at Afzal Ganj near the Osmania Hospital. It was encroached upon by lorries and trucks reducing the carriageway to just seventeen feet. After creating parking facilities for heavy vehicles at the Jail Compound, we announced that all lorries and trucks should be removed from the road. There was no response. Two days later we employed a crane which started lifting the trucks and lorries to the designated place. Transporters and city leaders howled in protest and threatened that they would complain to the chief minister and the prime minister. The chief minister did not see them. The operation was started at eight am and was over in two hours. I went to a nearby shop and rang up the chief minister to report that the operation was over. He patted me over the phone.

During my spell in the municipal corporation, I had seen every nook and corner of the city. I had provided municipal services in hitherto inaccessible areas and won public acclaim. I attended literary and general functions in the heart of the old city. Sometimes grievances of the citizens of the old city were satisfied merely by my attending one of their social functions.

My earlier acquaintance of the city was deepened by my spell in the corporation and, that in return, enhanced my love for it.

I could write a whole book on my tenure in the corporation.

Before leaving the corporation, I had Vengala Rao inaugurate two gardens. Indira Park was laid where a swamp existed. Sanjeevayya Park was laid as a rose garden on the foreshore of Hussain Sagar Lake. In his speech at the public function, Vengala Rao paid glowing tributes to me and said that more significant work had been done in the last three years than in its entire history.[9]

***

[9] *The Indian Express*, Monday, 12 September 1977

GENE AND MEME

Every day I returned home to a depressing scene created by Rahul's addiction. There is no dearth of gratuitous, well-meaning advice from close relations, friends and even strangers who themselves have no clue about dealing with an addict. While we listened to all that crap quietly, we tried to analyze whether there had been some deficiency in our upbringing of Rahul.

Once, Bindi casually complained to my mother about my lack of demonstrative emotional behaviour towards her. 'Not surprising,' was my mother's laconic reply, 'he is his father's son!'

My mother's double censure of her husband and son set me on a mental journey to my past. Whereas my childhood was spent in warm family relationships, my parents observed studied economy when it came to praising, kissing and hugging their children. I have a vivid memory of a particular incident. One morning, as I was reading *The Tribune*, I jumped up suddenly. My father was sitting in an easy chair about five feet away from me. He asked me the cause of the excitement. I replied that I had stood first-in-first in BA honours examination in the university. He smiled and said, 'Very good!' That was all. He did not get up and embrace me; he did not even pat me. After some time when my mother came home from outside, my father told her about my result. She said beamingly that she had always believed that would happen, and then she gave me a pat on the back.

That lack of exhibition of warmth in the parental recognition of my achievement was very frustrating for me. I felt as if I had failed the exam. I felt so depressed that later that evening I quietly slipped away to the riverside and sat there a long time contemplating suicide by jumping into the river. I played with pebbles, throwing them in the river as far as I could. Then I dipped my hand in the cold water. That calmed me down and I returned home to a quiet dinner.

I was aware of this deficient trait in my parents and I tried to make up for that in my behaviour with my children. Obviously my efforts had not been able to offset my genetic legacy adequately.

A Double Whammy

Generally, one of the spouses often makes up for the deficiencies of the other. In our case, Bindi turned out to be a shade worse than me in that respect. She had spent her childhood years away from her parents in a missionary school hostel. She came to stay with her parents after she had finished her school. She told me that whenever her father returned home in the evening, children would slink away to their respective rooms and emerge only when summoned for dinner. There too there was no mirth, not even talking. This was in contrast to my family where meals were occasions to share the day's happenings, to pull each other's leg and indulge in banter.

After our marriage, in keeping with the contemporary fad promoted by commercial companies and medical opinion, and much against my mother's advice, Bindi weaned away our children from breastfeeding before time and put them on milk bottles. Bottle feeding could easily be passed on to maids or even to male servants. Bindi kept a crib next to her bed into which the infant could be shoved. She told me she did not know any bedtime stories to tell children. Thereupon I took on that duty. When my mother visited us, she would supplement my efforts at storytelling. So, Bindi's bonding with the children left a lot to be desired. At that time American comics were the rage for growing children. So, as our children came into that group, storytelling became a self-help activity through comics.

In Hyderabad, we stayed in a spacious house in Bashir Bagh. Now that plot houses the headquarters of the police commissioner. At that time, there were about twenty trees in the backyard of the house with a fountain in the centre. As soon as I returned from office, I would take off my clothes, put on swimming trunks, and get into the fountain pool along with Rahul and Sandhya. They used to love it. Initially Bindi, who sat ready with tea and snacks, objected to our 'rowdyism'. In response, we splashed water on her, spoiling her starched cotton sari. Gradually, she came around to accept our rowdy behaviour but never joined us.

We had a swing tied to the big neem tree in our backyard and everyone could enjoy swinging in that. We also kept a pet dog, a big tortoise and a deer in the compound. It was also traditional in my parents' house for adults to play the game of 'Hide-and-Seek' with children on most evenings. I kept that up and even my mother whenever she was with us would join. I too played that game with my grandchildren till recently.

However, Bindi and I were too involved in our respective jobs. Sandhya later recalled some instances of our attitude which hurt her. Once she went up on stage in her school for her first debate for which she had prepared really hard. She felt frustrated when she noticed that unlike others, her parents were not in the audience. Later, she took part in a play, and again we were missing because it was in the middle of our working day.

Today, as I write this and look back, I feel that our nuclear family was deficient in physical bonding. While genes might offer some explanation for that, it cannot be held as a justification, and emotional patterns can certainly be changed by deliberate action.

Rahul frequently held it against us that we had left him with my parents when we went to England in 1964. Though they had a very happy time with the grandparents, the unique place reserved only for parents remained empty for over a year. Children can experience 'abandonment' at that stage of their life; they do not have the understanding that it is a temporary phase, and their minds do not process this absence in the same way as older persons can.

On Hugs

When I was posted in Delhi during 1980-1982, Rahul stayed back in Hyderabad. We really could not do anything about his decisions. He joined us later in Delhi. One early evening I saw him lying flat on his bed. There was something about his pained vacant look that made me feel a sudden surge of pity for him. I asked him what he was thinking about. 'Nothing,' he said. 'Nobody thinks of nothing anytime,' I said. Then I sat down by his side and drew him towards me. He made that easy by his readiness to be lifted up. I embraced him. He too gave me an answering hug and started sobbing. Happiness is an unexpected hug. I realized at that moment that both of us needed more of such hugs. That evening I felt the pain of Rahul's loneliness. He was caught in a vicious circle. He was lonely because of his addiction; he was addicted because of his loneliness. Not entirely, said a pang in my heart. How much was our contribution to that? We did not know how to break out of that *chakravyuh*.

*

Rahul used to come home very late and sometimes did not return at night. We came to accept that. In fact, the period of his absence gave us some peace. However, at the back of our minds, there was a nagging worry about his whereabouts and well-being. If the phone rang late at night, our immediate fear was that it might be some bad news about him.

Once, his company sent him to Vijayawada for a copywriting assignment for a client. He was completely drunk when he left home to catch the bus for Vijayawada. I pleaded with him not to go but he did not listen to me. I then spoke to the superintendent of police of Vijayawada, Dr Naik, and requested him to have him picked up and sent home. When a police officer went to the lodge in which Rahul was staying, he asked him under what authority of law he was being picked up. The officer told him politely that I was not well and so his presence was needed at home. He resisted being shoved into a jeep but was too drunk to do much. He lost that job and blamed me for that.

Later, I spoke to the director general of police and requested his help to have Rahul arrested off the record and kept in the lockup for a night. That might put some fear of God in him. The DGP sent an inspector of police to my house. The inspector went to Rahul's room and talked to him for some time. Rahul asked him the same question that he had asked the police in Vijayawada and stayed put.

In October 1985 I went for my heart bypass surgery to Houston.

After my operation, we visited various places including Los Angeles and New Jersey. Whenever we were in a mood and condition to go out, our host Ashok Jha, a junior service colleague of mine, would drive us to Washington. His charming wife, Sona, would pack a lunch for us. There Bindi underwent a cataract operation of the left eye.

While convalescing we had a good holiday and saw some interesting parts of America.

Returning home on 10 January 1986 we saw what havoc had been wrought in our house during our absence. Rahul had the free run of the house and indulged unchecked in his revelries. Sandhya had no peace at all.

***

Agro and Beyond

From the municipal corporation I was transferred to agro-industries corporation. Vengala Rao told me, 'The chairman and MD are always bickering. Go and do something.'

As I drove into a dreary compound, I was greeted by striking employees of the corporation. They had been on strike for over a fortnight. I called their leader and told him that it was not fair to greet me that way. 'Let me settle down and look into their problems.' He agreed.

I then went and called on the chairman, M. Narayan Reddy. He was a genial and knowledgeable person and a senior Congress leader representing Nizamabad. He had also been Member of Parliament and we had known each other in a general way. He got up in a shuffle, looked at me in confusion and then said that I was the first MD to step into his room. I too was surprised at that.

We agreed on some ground rules. There should not be any cliques in the corporation. We would sort out any difference of opinion quietly instead of indulging in spats on files.

The whole office wore a depressed look with curtains hanging loosely from strings. The board room looked like a taluk office. The salaries of officers were low and their travelling allowances were so meagre that nobody could afford to stay in any town overnight

– much less in places like Mumbai and Delhi. Their morale was low. I was surprised to learn that whenever the chairman fixed a board meeting, my predecessor would proceed on a tour. Every fortnight he would write to the government highlighting the wasteful expenditure incurred by the chairman and recommend the abolition of the post. The chairman, in his turn, would recount the irresponsible behaviour of the MD and ask for his transfer.

Since its inception ten years before, the corporation had been incurring mounting losses. I called a meeting of the senior officers and asked each one of them to submit a note on the nature of the work of the division under him and his assessment of its potential. On the basis of their suggestions and my own appraisal, I drew up the annual corporate plan and fixed a target of a profit of one million rupees. Alongside, a proposal for the overhaul of salary and travelling allowance was approved by the board.

Bonanza for Staff

The first reaction to the bonanza came from the employees' union. Its demands had been more than met and I told them in jest that they should elect me as their president. I thought their president had come to thank me. Instead, he protested saying that my action dealt a severe blow to trade unionism. The proper course should have been for the union to strike and then for me to do what I had done by way of conceding their demands!

That was another lesson in practical life for me!

The corporation closed the year with a cash profit of Rs 0.99 million – just Rs 10,000 short of the target we had fixed. It was its first cash profit.

One day a file came to me for my approval for the continuation of the services of a lawyer who was fighting a court case filed against the corporation by the State Trading Corporation of India (STC). It had imported sulphur for a subsidiary of our corporation of which also I was the MD. The corporation had defaulted in payment to STC which thereupon filed a suit for recovery. It was being contested by the agro-industries corporation. Out of a claim of Rs 1.3 million, more than half was by way of penal interest.

Seeing no point in contesting the case, I ordered termination of the service of the lawyer. Next, I went to Delhi and met the commerce secretary, the late P.C. Alexander, explained the case to him and proposed that if the suit against our corporation was dropped and the penal interest waived, I would repay the principal in three quarterly instalments. He found the proposal reasonable, and was good enough to speak to the chairman of STC accordingly. The latter accepted my offer. My chairman was thrilled and proposed a special vote of thanks to me in the next meeting of the board of the corporation.

*

Dr Channa Reddy became chief minister for the second time on 6 March 1978. He asked me to take over the Municipal Corporation of Hyderabad once again because the leaders of the city wanted my return. I was very flattered but declined saying I did not consider it a good practice to go back to a job one had left behind. He was not happy with my reply.

Leather Corporation

As it happened, in January 1979 I was selected as chairman and managing director of Bharat Leather Corporation under the government of India. Channa Reddy suspected that to be the reason for my declining his offer. It was clear that I had incurred Channa Reddy's displeasure.

I was misled about the nature of the new job. The brief sent to me stated that the leather corporation was to be in charge of the total development of the leather industry in the country including its export, and that the headquarters of the corporation would be shifted from Agra to Delhi.

There was no reason for the leather corporation to be located in Agra. Also, the export of leather and its products was centralized in the State Trading Corporation which was under the commerce ministry. Any plan for the integrated development of the leather industry had to cover exports too. The commerce ministry would not give up its turf.

I was, however, able to set up a camp office in Delhi. From there, I tried to make the best out of a bad bargain.

The variety of ethnic footwear made in different states of India is fascinating. The desi *jooti* of the Hindi belt, the *mojras* of Bengal, the variety of *chappals* special to Kolhapur, Cuttack and Bengal and the knitted sandals of Chamba in Himachal are some of the attractions. The problem is the lack of standardization of sizes and of quality. We collected samples of local footwear from all over the country and invited representatives of manufacturers for a meeting. I offered to help them to standardize the sizes and upgrade the quality of their products. After that we would buy their product in bulk for the chain of the new emporia which were planned all over the country, and also for export. Imagine my frustration when they said that they would lose their unique attraction if they were standardized.

I prepared a master plan for the comprehensive development of the leather industry in the country. I was able to establish the corporation's flagship project, an emporium in Connaught Place.

All in all, from the professional angle, my stint in the Bharat Leather Corporation was a waste of time.

A Hidden Ghost

When Sandhya was a schoolgirl, we used to feel that she was somewhat withdrawn. In the beginning we thought she might be a studious and introvert child, but as time passed it became worrisome. She was more than merely introvert; she was visibly knotted up. I felt that she was carrying some burden which she did not want to share with us. She never asked us for anything and was reluctant to accept anything we offered. One day when we pressed her to explain why she was such a closed book, she shocked us by telling us that she had been sexually abused during the period of our stay in England when both Rahul and she had been left behind in the care of my parents. Initially, we dismissed it as one of those little games which children play. Sandhya insisted that we try and understand that it was not one of those games but real abuse by someone who was close to the family. We were naturally horrified and shaken up by her revelation. Her innocent face at the tender age of five kept on haunting us. We could not believe what horrors she had endured quietly without letting anyone in the family know. The abuser had blackmailed her that if she told us about the abuse, we would blame her and even disown her for being so wicked. She therefore suffered quietly in guilt-ridden lonesome silence. The abuse lasted over five years in Delhi and stopped only when we relocated to Hyderabad.

Was it the tyranny of the dark secret lodged in her innocent breast that kept her so 'knotted up'? Was that the reason that in her early childhood she had become a reclusive bookworm? She was always lying in a corner with some book by the philosopher Jiddu Krishnamurti. Before she finished her school, she had read all his books.

Later, when she had shifted to Delhi to be on her own, she faced considerable difficulty in finding independent accommodation as a 'single woman' in New Delhi. In one particular place the landlords harassed her, and she had to file a complaint with the police. However, she did not tell me about it. Compared to Hyderabad, Delhi is a relatively harsh place to navigate, and she had gone from driving her own car in Hyderabad to relying on public transport in Delhi. When she told us about the constant harassment women face in public places, we did not take it seriously. However, after some time, I bought her a car and that made a lot of difference.

She landed good jobs in Delhi. She also became involved in social justice activism including empowerment of women. But despite her busy schedule, she could not close up on Rahul. His shadow continued to chase her. It was sheer luck that one of her friends, Sujata, was a recovering alcoholic and opened Sandhya's eyes to the idea of alcoholism as a disease and the possibility of recovery from it. Sandhya then introduced Bindi and me to AA (Alcoholics Anonymous), and encouraged us to attend a meeting or meet some people from AA so we could get support in dealing with Rahul's alcoholism.

However, she was relieved to be away from the family obsessed with Rahul and his bottle. For the next seven years Sandhya did not visit Hyderabad. Bindi and I used to visit her for a month most winters and she made our stay as comfortable as possible.

***

Mother of all Solutions

In 1987, on professional advice, we sent Rahul to the National Institute of Mental Health and Neuro Sciences (NIMHANS) at Bengaluru. Now it is a university.

After about a month, I paid a visit to the institute. Rahul was somewhat active and cheerful but his movements were not monitored and he went anywhere he liked.

I discovered the reason for his good cheer when Rahul introduced me to a charming young girl named Rajeshwari, and asked me what I thought of her. She was pretty and had an innocent moon-face look. He told me what I was anticipating – he had fallen in love with her. I felt a surge of sympathy for her.

Rahul stayed there for over two months. After some time Bindi and I were asked to visit the place for a fortnight so that the psychiatrist in charge of Rahul's case could have joint sessions with us before Rahul's discharge. We stayed there from 12 to 27 April 1987. They gave us a big room in which the three of us had to stay together in considerable discomfort. Bindi used to cook in the same room on days we did not go out to eat.

Rahul was discharged at the end of our visit. I had just acquired a new Maruti car and had driven in that from Hyderabad to Bengaluru. It was the rage of the country at that time. I thought that Rahul would like to drive that on our homeward journey. Surprisingly, he did not show any excitement and took the wheel as if he was being forced to do so. A short distance out of Bengaluru there was a showdown between Rahul and us on some point.

*

Whenever any matrimonial proposal for Rahul was made to us, I used to explain Rahul's problem and ask to be excused. However, soon after his return from Bengaluru, Rahul himself broached the topic. Folk wisdom holds that marriage is a panacea for many aberrations. However, we were not in favour of Rahul's marriage without first sorting out his addiction problem. That would not have been fair to any girl or her family. I decided to take similar action in this case although it was a love affair.

On one of my trips to Delhi, I went to see Rajeshwari in her college hostel. There I spent about two hours with her telling her all about Rahul's addiction. For her own sake, I tried to dissuade her from getting married to Rahul. I warned her mother also against such a prospect. Both heard me patiently but said that Rajeshwari was confident that she would be able to bring Rahul back to normalcy. I could see that like us, Rajeshwari's family was also blissfully innocent about the nature of drug addiction.

The wedding took place at New Delhi on 14 February 1988 at a simple ceremony at a temple in accordance with Rahul's wishes.

Rahul had a good job in an advertising firm in Delhi and so the couple stayed in Delhi after their marriage. Rajeshwari too got a job and we thought they would live there happily. Whenever we asked her about how things were going she tried to cover up the real situation and gave us a favourable report. However, whenever I visited them in Delhi, I did not get that impression. There was a dismal air about their flat. At last I found out what I had feared. Rahul did not have a job and Rajeshwari was managing the house somehow. I then told Rajeshwari that I would take care of the house rent without telling Rahul so that he didn't take that for granted. During my occasional visits to Delhi, I used to visit them and even stay with them.

The normal ambience of a newly married couple's house – the warm hymeneal glow, conjugal argot, teasing and laughing, humming of tunes while attending to domestic chores, discussion of the day's accounts, going to movies or concerts – a million pixels which make up the picture of a new couple – was missing. I did not get the feeling that I was staying with my son. I used to feel uncomfortable and even physically inconvenienced staying with them, especially when I had the option of staying in a deluxe suite of the Andhra Pradesh Bhavan. I also got the feeling that they were not enjoying my stay with them. That was despite Rajeshwari's best efforts to paper over the cracks in their marriage. She did not complain about anything.

In Delhi Rahul had intermittent jobs and whatever he earned, he spent on his addiction. He was often verbally and even physically abusive with Rajeshwari. She did not tell us anything presumably because she had got into the mess despite my warning. They also kept shifting houses and, at one point, stayed for a few months at her parents' house.

A daughter was born to them on 6 July 1990. Rahul and I went over a list of names and agreed on 'Raisa' as a name for her. She turned out to be a smiling child. We did not ever see her cry.

One day Rajeshwari opened up to me and I was horrified to learn that Rahul had only sunk deeper in his addiction.

Four years had passed since their marriage. Rahul had no steady job and Rajeshwari was somehow managing with her salary supplemented by our subsidy.

***

Under a Super Star

On my return from Delhi, Chief Minister T. Anjaiah posted me to his favourite department – labour. At that time, he himself was close to his removal. His fault was that he had overdone the welcome to Rajiv Gandhi on his visit to Hyderabad as general secretary of the Congress party. Rajiv Gandhi snubbed him publicly for wasting money on erecting too many welcome arches in his honour.

As labour secretary I had five departments under me and each of them had a separate minister. I therefore used to refer to myself as a 'male Draupadi – in labour'!

Abolitions and Mergers

After about six months, on Anjaiah's exit, I was transferred to the newly created department of public enterprises as its director general and ex-officio secretary in the industries department. There I worked out a scheme of abolition and merger of over seventy overlapping corporations and boards in the state.

*

The quick parade of chief ministers between 1978 and 1983 caused first amusement and then anger amongst the people of Andhra

Pradesh. It was manifested in the massive victory won by the fledgling Telugu Desam Party in the elections of 1982. It won 202 seats out of 294 seats in the legislative assembly. Its leader, N.T. Rama Rao, popularly known as NTR, took over as chief minister on 1 January 1983.

NTR was a top actor in Telugu films. He had played the role of most Hindu mythological heroes besides lead roles in many social films with a variety of themes. He was a household name in the state and women in villages used to worship his image as a god in their homes. He captured the political stage on the wave of his enormous popularity.

In his election speeches, he had been declaring, amongst other things, that he would reduce the plethora of corporations and boards. The chief secretary told him that I had prepared a note on the subject. Turning a customary courtesy call into a business meeting, he said, 'Very good. Tell me about your proposals.'

I had the papers with me. I started, 'Sir, I think that the number of corporations could be easily reduced from seventy to twenty-three.'

'No,' he said, 'it should be thirteen.'

I replied, 'I have worked it out and have arrived at this number…'

'Let me see,' he interrupted me. I gave him a copy of the list of the corporations and boards. He started reading out aloud and then came to 'housing'. I had proposed abolitions and mergers from nine corporations/boards to three. Suddenly he said, 'Warehousing corporation should also be merged with the housing corporation.'

I submitted that warehousing had nothing in common with housing corporation.

'Why,' he cut me short, '*housing* is common!'

I tried to explain the difference between the two. He asked me to examine the matter further and meet him again.

*

NTR was used to solving problems in a span of three hours – average length of a Telugu movie. Life off-screen was not as simple. He had no understanding of the complexities of political and social issues. It was therefore a big job for the bureaucracy to adjust to his style of working. The first problem was his working hours. His official day started at five in the morning. He summoned senior officers from that time onwards and also gave appointments early in the morning to those wishing to meet him.

He had some eccentricities. Once he started wearing a ring in one ear, then he donned saffron robes and a turban in the style of Swami Vivekananda. There were rumours that he wore a sari at night.

Even in official meetings if someone brought out the implications and risks involved in any of his policy ideas, NTR would stand up and remind the small gathering that he was the representative of six-and-a-half crore Andhras! Ministers never opened their mouths before him although they were fully briefed. Secretaries had to do whatever talking was required and thus expose themselves to his displeasure.

NTR took some ill-advised and unpopular measures like reducing the age of retirement of government servants and banning private practice by government doctors. Doctors went on strike against the ban and the high court struck down the government orders. NTR not only lost face but also suffered an immediate slump in his popularity.

Health and Medicine

In September 1983 I was promoted as principal secretary and posted to the health and medical department. It was good to go to a running concern after a long time.

The health and medical department is manpower and capital intensive. The large number of physicians and surgeons are very influential. Every minister had some favourite doctor of his and so appeals and recommendations for transfers and postings were aplenty. My minister spent all his time playing with transfers and postings. After watching this spectacle for a few weeks, I issued orders that files relating to transfers should not come to me but be submitted directly to him.

A Coup and Restoration

Seven months after NTR became chief minister, he was advised a heart bypass surgery and so he went to Houston in the US. Immediately after his departure, his trusted lieutenant and finance minister, Nadendla Bhaskara Rao, and my minister, Ramamuni Reddy, plotted a coup and the former staked a claim to form the ministry. An obliging governor, Ram Lal, swore him in as chief minister on 16 August 1984 on the condition that he secure a vote of confidence of the assembly within a month. A recuperating NTR rushed back from America to fight the perfidy. That was the time when NTR's son-in-law, Chandrababu Naidu, showed his political acumen and organizing ability. To prevent Bhaskara Rao from buying up his party MLAs, he took them all to Bengaluru and lodged them in a hotel under virtual house arrest. They were brought to Hyderabad in a caravan of buses straight to the Assembly Hall on 16 September 1984. Unable thus to muster a majority, Bhaskara Rao resigned and NTR got his job back. A new swearing-in ceremony was held in the Raj Bhavan. It being a holiday, my driver had not come. Since I was staying close to Raj Bhavan, I decided to drive myself to the Raj Bhavan. Coming out of the house I saw a huge crowd. It was swelling with every passing minute. It thickened as I neared the gate of the Raj Bhavan. All around me were people, angry at the coup and delirious with happiness at the triumph of justice. They wanted to witness the 'restoration' of their idol. On the railway track behind me a train had been stalled. People had climbed on the roof tops of the train's compartments. Caught right in the midst of jostling crowds, I could neither go ahead nor reverse. Some persons started making menacing gestures at me. Someone shouted, asking me who I was. Before I could reply from behind the locked window, somebody shouted, 'Arun Shourie'. He was a prominent journalist and a friend of NTR's party. I nodded in panic. Someone shouted, 'Let him go.' Suddenly I realized that my car was not under my control. It was floating as if in water. In a few seconds, I found myself lodged in front of the gate of the Raj Bhavan. The crowd had broken the police barricade and had gatecrashed into the compound of the Raj Bhavan. I drove the 100- metre stretch from the gate to reach the site of the swearing-in function.

The governor was complicit in the sordid drama. The Congress government at the Centre was hugely embarrassed. It quickly recalled the governor. Two months later NTR dissolved the legislative assembly and was returned to power for a full term. He ruled supreme till 1989.

*

There were 900 PHCs (primary health centres) in rural areas and they were largely without doctors because no doctor was willing to serve in rural areas. Those who went did not attend the centres but started private practice in nearby towns. Representations, recommendations and pressures came from all sides requesting cancellation of orders appointing their offspring or relatives in any PHC. Many graduates in medicine would try to get into postgraduate classes to escape such postings. After all, the parents of medical graduates had to make up for the huge capitation fees which they had paid for their admission. The rot is deep and widespread in the whole country. While nearly forty per cent of doctors in the US are Indians, back home there was a dearth of doctors.

I suggested enhanced salaries to doctors posted in the centres located in backward and tribal areas. NTR demurred but agreed. However, it had no effect.

World Humour Conference

I was involved in some social and cultural organizations. One of them was a humour society of Urdu writers and poets of Hyderabad. I remained its president for over two decades. We organised an annual weekend function of Urdu writers and poets with a separate session for prose, poetry and jokes.

In 1985 we enlarged its scope to cover all languages of India and some foreign languages too, and even non-verbal categories like cartoons, mime and puppetry. We called it 'World Humour Conference'. Fifteen countries including the USSR, the US, England, France, Japan and Pakistan participated in it besides all Indian states except Assam. Twenty-two languages were covered. Parallel sessions on Indian languages were hosted by different linguistic associations in Hyderabad. Leading cartoonists of India, mimicry and mime artists attended it. An exhibition of the best cartoons, screening of humour films, a session of jokes of the world were part of the festival.

Come to think of it, humour is such an important part of our life. The court jester enjoyed immunity against his actions and thus often was the only source of feedback for absolute rulers. No daily newspaper can go without the pocket cartoon on the front page. Most papers carry strip cartoons. In circus the bumbling joker is, in fact, an accomplished artiste. In the card games that I know, Joker trumps all other cards. The *Vidushak* in the Indian theatrical tradition and Shakespearean fools are generally clever commoners who use their wits to outdo people of higher social standing. It is not for nothing that humour – *Hasya rasa* – is one of the nine – *Nava rasas* – in the Indian theory of aesthetics.

I wanted Prime Minister Indira Gandhi to inaugurate the conference. P.V. Narasimha Rao who was then the home minister agreed to take me to her. Accordingly, I flew to Delhi on the morning of 31 October 1984.

As I landed at the Delhi airport, I heard that the prime minister had been assassinated.

Balram Jhakar, then speaker of the Lok Sabha, inaugurated it in February 1985. It was a huge success.

Bulgaria used to hold a biannual international meet on humour. Their delegation invited me for their forthcoming session at Gabrovo.

Gabrovo had a permanent museum of humorous paintings and sculptures in a palatial marble building. However, their proceedings were all in the Bulgarian language which the foreign delegates could not understand.

x+I = T

On my return from Bulgaria in March 1985, NTR called me and said that he wanted me to take over tourism. I said I was too senior to go to that job. He said, 'I have some ideas on the subject and I want you to execute them. Don't worry about the budget. I will sanction the budget based on your proposals.'

I introduced water sports in the Hussain Sagar utilizing the boats bought by the relief department for the cyclone of 1977 which were lying idle in godowns.

A project to develop Bhavani Island in the Krishna river at Vijayawada was prepared and it grew into a popular resort.

*

I am fascinated by tourism and its immense potential for development. We have only scratched the surface of our potential for tourism. It is an industry the raw materials of which are littered all over the country – and they are inexhaustible. In 1959 I had visited Kerala for the first time to attend the National Tourism Development Council. When I saw the backwaters I suggested that they should be 'exploited' by providing houseboats there. It took a generation before someone implemented the idea. Rocks are a fantastic feature of Hyderabad. They are 2,500 million years old and are our oldest physical heritage. With minimum investment they can be turned into tourist attractions. Instead they are being destroyed recklessly for short-term gains. In 1996 a group of us Hyderabadis established the Society to Save Rocks. I have been its president for twenty years and our members have been canvassing hard for the preservation of rocks.

Another problem with tourism in India is that its development is top-down instead of bottom-up. Local bodies take no interest in touristic places within their jurisdiction. State governments ask the government of India for funds to develop their tourist properties. There is too much dependence on government for the development of tourism. At the same time, an adequate appreciation of the potential for tourism is missing amongst governments. There are countries which depend on tourism for their survival. I foresee a situation in which the government role in tourism will 'wither away' and it will be replaced completely by private enterprise. The government should come in only selectively on projects like the development of the infrastructure or of special cases like the ruined city of Vijayanagar.

Over the years, I developed an algebraic equation for the development of tourism: T= x + I where 'T' stands for tourism, 'x' for anything, and 'I' for imagination. In other words, imagination applied to anything results in tourism. It is to be noted that 'x' is in lower case whereas 'I' is in the uppercase. That denotes their relative importance. Haryana had none of the traditional 'raw materials' of tourism. Yet it became a tourism state because of the imagination of S.K. Misra. Similarly, someone in Rajasthan came up with the concept of the 'Palace on Wheels' and the concept of 'desert' tourism.

I have expatiated on this equation a number of times in conferences and published articles.

A Morning Call

One early morning, my phone rang while I was still in deep sleep. I looked at the watch. It was five am. I picked up the receiver and grumbled a hello. The voice said, 'This is Rama Rao speaking.'

Rama Rao was one of my colleagues. I said, 'Rama Rao, what's happened? Why call so early in the morning?'

The tone turned authoritative as the voice announced, 'This is the chief minister speaking.'

Normally, some PA rings up and tells you that the chief minister is coming on the line. That gives you some time to gather your wits.

'Sorry, Sir, I did not recognize your voice on the phone.'

'Never mind,' he said sportingly and added, 'I wanted to tell you that I like your ideas on tourism.'

I could not understand the reason behind the call. However, it made my day. I thanked him for his kindness.

Meet the PM

During his visit to the US for his bypass surgery, NTR had seen Disneyland. On return, he wanted to set up an amusement park along similar lines. I told him that the import of equipment for amusement parks was banned. He said, 'We will get the policy relaxed. You go and meet the prime minister.' I said I was too small a fry to ask for an appointment with the prime minister. He said, 'You tell him that you represent the chief minister of Andhra Pradesh.' I took it as a joke and came out of the meeting.

A week later, I happened to be present in another meeting headed by him. Suddenly, he asked me, 'Have you been to Delhi?'

'What for, Sir?'

'I told you to go and meet the prime minister.'

His secretary, the late Raghavendra Rao, winked at me and told the chief minister that he would sort it out.

Ultimately, my minister, a lady, NTR's political adviser, the late Upendra, and I went to Delhi and met the minister of state for finance. As soon as Upendra started explaining the object of our visit, the minister said, 'Now what does Mr Drama Rao want?'

That ended the meeting. I don't know what report Upendra gave to NTR. The subject was never raised again.

***

Revisiting the Devil

On the personal front, Rahul's addiction had peaked. It haunted us every living moment and singed many occasions of happiness.

Noting the worsening situation in Rahul and Rajeshwari's life in Delhi, we brought them to Hyderabad in April 1992. By that time, I had retired from service and we had moved to our own house in Banjara Hills. Rajeshwari got a job in the Apollo Hospital as director of nursing and Rahul got one in the company which he had worked for before. His boss, Neelamegham, was a genial and understanding person.

Dialogues with Child

The small family stayed with us. I used to narrate bedtime stories to Raisa as I had done with her father a long time ago. She was a bundle of delight. Even Bindi, who is not very fond of children, started doting on her as I had never seen her do before. We were always buying small gifts for her or taking her out for picnics. When I sat on the deck of our house early mornings, Raisa would suddenly emerge from the bedroom and jump onto my lap. She would share the plate of papaya which I eat regularly as a part of my breakfast. We would talk about a variety of things. Some crows, sparrows and other birds would fly around and sometimes perch close to us. She would ask me all sorts of questions and I answered her to the best of my ability. Our conversations were so interesting that once I wrote an article based only on one morning chat between us. It was broadcast on the All India Radio and its translations were published in leading Hindi and Urdu magazines. My sessions with her were very insightful for me and I was surprised that I learnt so much from a little child. I never applied any censor on her queries. Our bond grew stronger.

Children should never be fobbed off with evasive replies to their queries. They are the sort of questions our scriptures and philosophers raise and try to answer. Children are very eager listeners and one learns a lot in trying to answer their innocent questions.

I am so glad I put aside everything for her. I wish I had done as much for my children. We played games together. She would play my wife and pretend to go out for shopping leaving her imaginary children in my care with appropriate instructions. Sometimes she played an officer with me as a petitioner. I wondered wherefrom she had picked up all the information to play the make-believe roles. I became her virtual father. She insisted on sleeping with us.

We used to celebrate her birthdays with great enthusiasm and tried to give her as normal a life as possible. Sometimes she saw Rahul in an aggressive mood, shouting at us. She would then come and hide behind the door in our bedroom. We tried to protect her from such scenes and appealed to Rahul not to do so for her sake. He did not care even though he loved her. Maybe he was far more helpless in his fight against the addiction than we imagined. Today, I know that addiction affects physically and emotionally too and the alcoholic has problems expressing that. Sometimes when Rahul was in a nasty mood, Rajeshwari too moved into our bedroom.

Aside from such episodes, I think Raisa had a seemingly happy childhood. She developed the habit of reading very early in her life and would sometimes spend hours under a table reading a book. Her other favourite pass-time was holding 'fashion pageants' for her dolls in which all of us used to participate. Rajeshwari too tried to spend as much time with her as she could after returning from work. In fact, Rajeshwari's entire life revolved around Raisa. She tried to create an ambience of normalcy for her. Rajeshwari participated in all the events in her school. She was most concerned that Rahul's addiction should not affect Raisa's normal growth. She even took Raisa's teachers into confidence and requested them not to ask her any questions about her father.

About two years passed in this manner.

Divorce

Our sympathies were with Rajeshwari and Raisa. Not finding any prospect of improvement we discussed the possibility of a divorce. After mulling over the idea for a few days, Rajeshwari agreed that for the sake of her daughter, divorce from Rahul would be the best solution. I took her to my friend and a leading senior advocate, Habib Ansari.

One day in 1994, Rahul drank so much that he could not get up the next morning. He was lying in his bedroom and I was busy with my work. Suddenly, my friend K. Umapathy rang me up and, without any preliminary small talk, asked me: 'Where is your son?'

'Why? He is in his room.'

'Are you sure?' he asked.

'I think so. I saw him there a few minutes ago.'

'Just check again.'

I peeped into the room and did not find Rahul there. 'Well,' Umapathy said, 'he has met with an accident close to your house. I have removed him to the Apollo Hospital. He is being attended to. Please reach the hospital.'

'I hope he is dead,' I muttered to myself. That would remove our daily suffering once and for all. It would be better than the daily torture.

Having finished his stock of alcohol, Rahul had gone out on his bike to buy some more. While returning, he hit a doctor's car head on and was grievously injured. I thought that the poor doctor would be hauled up for negligent driving. So I gave him a letter with a copy to the police that the doctor was not at fault.

Rahul had broken his femur bones and suffered multiple fractures in both legs. A prolonged operation was done and Rahul was discharged after a few days. We readied his room and sat down around him to cheer him up. He was not able to get up from his bed and had to be helped for every movement. We hoped that the accident would teach him a lesson and might bring him back to sobriety. But he showed no sign of remorse. He was rude to everyone in different ways. After about a month he was given a pair of crutches and a physiotherapist started teaching him how to use them. That gave him a measure of independence in his movement to go to the bathroom. We were satisfied on one point – he was not drinking or using any drugs. But we were mistaken. The network of the junkies is very strong and efficient. He had simply moved from alcohol to ganja and other dry stuff. His 'supplies' were somehow reaching him though he appeared normal to us. I don't know who arranged the money to pay for them. I learnt later that the couriers were some bearers of the Secunderabad Club. They used to push the packets from the window which opened outside into the compound of the house. That could be done without any one of us noticing them.

Rahul flew into a rage when he received the notice from the court for his counter to Rajeshwari's petition for divorce. He was still an invalid.

The judge asked Rajeshwari where she was staying. She replied that she was staying with her in-laws. 'It looks so odd,' he commented, 'you are filing a case for divorce against your husband and you are staying with his parents!' The whole court room and the galleries were filled with warring in-laws involved in divorce cases and here was a young woman alone with her lawyer asking for nothing by way of alimony, but only a release from a relationship gone wrong.

Rajeshwari replied coolly, 'Your Honour, my in-laws are different. They are *with* me, not with their son.' Rahul did not – indeed could not – file a counter or appear in the court. The divorce was granted ex-parte on 28 February 1995 – seven years to the day of the marriage.

Habib Ansari refused to take any fees. Shortly thereafter, he was elevated to the bench.

After the divorce, we told Rajeshwari that since she had ceased to be our daughter-in-law, we would adopt her as our daughter and that she would continue to stay with us. 'Moreover,' I added, 'if ever in the future, you happen to find a suitable man and like him, we will gladly perform your marriage.' With suppressed tears, she thanked us but said that in the changed circumstances, she could not stay with us. We said that we would throw out Rahul as soon as he regained his mobility and she would continue to stay with us without any embarrassment. She said: 'How can that be. What will the world say?'

'Why not?' I said. Bindi added, 'Damn the world. We don't care.'

Rajeshwari stayed with us for a few weeks and we liked that arrangement. Our magnet was Raisa. We had grown very fond of her and could not imagine her going anywhere away from us. Then, despite our pleadings, Rajeshwari decided to go back to her parents in Delhi. We kept in regular touch with her. Raisa used to dream about us and get up and not find us around. She was beginning to distinguish between dream and reality.

After a few months, Rajeshwari's father retired from service and they decided to settle down in Hyderabad. Rajeshwari and Raisa came back with them. They took up a flat down the same road in Banjara Hills where we were staying. We used to visit them every evening.

Three more years passed that way. Looking back, I wonder how we managed to retain our sanity without resorting to temples and 'holy men'.

***

Some Coincidences

Sometimes simple coincidences can make great differences in one's life. Let me mention some of them.

Those days the birth anniversary of Mohammad Quli Qutb Shah, founder of Hyderabad and the first anthologized Urdu poet of India, used to be celebrated at the Qutb Shahi tombs.

I attended them regularly, but somehow I could not attend it in 1987. In her presidential address the governor, Ms Kumudben Joshi, observed that a fitting and lasting memorial to the founder of the city would be to publish his biography. Shashi S. Singh, director of the publications division of the government of India was a special guest of the function. He immediately responded by declaring to the cheers of the gathering that he would take up that job.

The following day he came to see me and requested me to write a biography of Mohammad Quli. Till then I had only had a dilettante's interest in the history and culture of Hyderabad and so I told Singh that I was not qualified to take up the job. He said he had consulted a number of persons and they had all suggested my name. I still did not agree. He followed up with reminders from Delhi while I kept on demurring.

In the Doghouse

In October 1987 I was suddenly transferred from Tourism because I had not obliged a son-in-law of NTR in a trivial case. I was posted to the department of rehabilitation. There was hardly any work in the department though it had the full complement of personal staff and other perks of a principal secretary.

It is strange how lack of work demoralizes a person. Hitherto I had generally held man-sized jobs and had enjoyed longer than average tenures. My new charge simply offered no such scope. For about a month I came regularly to office and opened my shop but there was no customer throughout the day. I was getting out of practice with my signature.

One day I went over my situation and found that I had been dumped merely on the basis of a baseless complaint. No fault had been found with me. I had seen quite a number of my friends and colleagues passing through such phases in their career. Such fate had befallen me rather late in my career. NTR's secretary, P.L. Sanjeeva Reddy, suggested that I should come and see the chief minister and just request for a change. I could not bring myself to do that.

I then decided to accept Singh's offer of writing the biography of the founder of the city.

In a period of eighteen months that I spent in that sinecure, I did two books: one was my travelogue of America in Urdu titled *Hawai Columbus*. In 1492 Christopher Columbus had gone by sea in the wrong direction and thus accidentally discovered America. I was the second Columbus and I had gone by air! The book was illustrated by Sandhya's friend Ute Krause. She was a well-known young German illustrator. She was spending a summer with us and was paid in terms of unlimited quantities of Hyderabadi mangoes – a remuneration she was entirely thrilled with. A number of its chapters were serialized in the *Siasat* daily and it was well received in India and Pakistan.

The other book was Mohammad Quli's biography. I gave it the title of *Prince Poet Lover Builder*. My research gave me a good grounding in the history of Hyderabad which was to become my specialization later.

It was also to launch me into a career of full-time writing. Indeed, sweet are the fruits of adversity!

The book was released by Dr Shankar Dayal Sharma, then vice president of India, at the Raj Bhavan in Hyderabad. In my introduction, I said that the book was written when I was in Siberia. At tea after the function, Sharma asked me what had taken me to Siberia. When I explained that it was a metaphor for my posting, he laughed and said, 'Not a high price to pay for authorship!'

*

The second coincidence brought into fruition a proposal for the Sound and Light programme at the Golkonda Fort which had not been accepted by the government of India for over a quarter of a century. In the good old days Hyderabad used to have the tradition of '*chowki* dinner'. It comprised a low table around which eight diners sat on a durrie spread on the ground and covered with a white sheet called *chandni*. The cuisine for the dinner was authentic Mughlai. I revived that and arranged it on the large platform around the mausoleum of Mohammad Quli's. We named it 'Dinner with the Founder of Hyderabad'. The mausoleum was flood-lit and the dinner was preceded by a ten-minute video programme on the tombs and followed by a short entertainment programme. It became very popular especially with the emerging corporate sector.

Sound & Light

When Rajiv Gandhi was the prime minister, he made training compulsory for all officers and even ministers.

One day I received a call from the prime minister's office. A group of eight ministers and secretaries were in 'retreat' at the Administrative College of India at Hyderabad. They were bored. Could I help?

I invited them for 'Dinner with the Founder'. It happened to be a full-moon night. Amongst the group was the minister of state for finance named Gadvi. During the dinner, he looked up at the Bala Hissar building perched at the highest point in the Golkonda Fort. Moonlight gave it a gentle soft glow. Gadvi turned to me and said, 'I say, you should start a sound and light programme at the fort.'

I jumped up and said, 'Sir, our proposal for that has been lying with the ministry of tourism for a long time. The financial adviser of the ministry has raised objections to the proposal on the ground that it is not financially viable.'

Gadvi replied, 'In such cases the financial viability should be given a broader interpretation taking the spin-off benefits into consideration.'

I could not believe my ears. He was speaking my language. 'Sir that is exactly how we have been arguing in our proposal.'

He said, 'Can you come and see me in Delhi next Monday?'

I reached his office accordingly.

In my presence he rang up the financial adviser of the tourism ministry. He mentioned the proposal.

I could only imagine what the voice on the phone said. But I heard the minister say, 'I am not asking for your opinion. You write whatever you like on the file and send it to me.'

Gadvi told me that he could sanction only up to fifty lakhs. For more funds, the proposal would have to go to the expenditure finance committee.

I did not want to risk a referral to a committee. I took the money hoping to persuade the state government to cough up the balance.

But that was not the end of the problem.

*

The Golkonda Fort is under the watch of the Archaeological Survey of India (ASI). It raised an objection that the Sound and Light project would damage the fort.

I requested for an appointment with K.P. Singh Deo, the Union minister of culture. I was told to join him on his forthcoming visit to the fort. I explained our proposal and wondered how the fort, exposed to the elements and open to vandals and encroachers for centuries, could be damaged by coloured lights and the sound of a commentary.

After the tour, the minister told the ASI officer to facilitate the project.

The state government also released the balance amount.

*

The electorate punished NTR for not having been fair to me. He lost the elections in November 1989 and Channa Reddy became chief minister for the second time on 3 December 1990. He pulled me out of the doghouse and shoved me into a slightly better kennel. I was posted as commissioner of the Institute of Training. He had not excused me for declining his offer of a second term in the municipal corporation.

I tried some of my pet theories of training at the cost of the trainees. I invited some real big names from different fields rather than departmental heads for lecturing to trainees. Good training should equip one to deal with the future across the existing frontiers rather than give a peep into how things were done in the past. Our training system lags behind the fast-changing realities of life around us.

Hyderabad 400

Hyderabad was going to be 400 years old in 1991. Someone suggested that the event should be celebrated. Channa Reddy called a meeting to which I was also invited. At the meeting various suggestions were made. At the end of the meeting a high-power committee was constituted with the chief minister as the chairman and me as the executive vice chairman.

I got down to drafting the pattern and content of the comprehensive celebrations. However, before the next meeting, Channa Reddy was replaced by N. Janardhana Reddy as chief minister. He had known me during my early days of glory as a young sub-collector in Gudur.

I was getting close to fifty-eight which was then the age of superannuation. As it happened, the chief secretary went abroad on leave. I was appointed to the post. I therefore retired as chief secretary on 31 March 1991.

Janardhana Reddy was very enthusiastic about the fourth centenary celebration of the city. For that purpose, he extended my service for a year. We made good progress in drafting the pattern of celebrations. It provided me an opportunity to expand and deepen my research base of the history and culture of Hyderabad. I proposed that the government should take advantage of the opportunity afforded by the celebration to address some of the perennial grievances of the old city about the neglect of its civic needs. This could be done by a release of Rs 400 crore worth of development programmes for the old city. For that purpose, I requested all the secretaries of government departments to pool their projects relating to the old city. We were thus able to come up with a package of Rs 400 crore worth of projects without any extra cost.

On the celebratory side, the highlight was a procession of forty tableaux each based on a significant milestone in the history of the city. They included highlighting of little known but inspiring incidents like the installation of the idols of Rama, Lakshmana and Sita by the Third Nizam of Hyderabad in the first Kayasth temple of Hyderabad in 1812. The plan was that the procession of forty tableaux mentioned above would start from the Golkonda Fort and end at the Charminar, a distance of eight kilometres. The procession would march past the prime minister who would be at Charminar. The passing out of the last tableau would coincide with sunset when, with the pressing of a button by the prime minister, 10,000 lamps would light up the Charminar and buildings around it. The prime minister would then address the audience, inaugurate the celebrations and announce the package of Rs 400 crore worth of projects – one crore each for a year of the life of the city.

The event attracted international interest and media teams from the BBC, ABC and the German TV sought permission to cover it. It would have been the most memorable spectacle Hyderabad had ever seen. Unfortunately, some old freedom fighters complained to the prime minister that we were glorifying the Nizam. P.V. Narasimha Rao called off his visit to Hyderabad. The programme was thus cancelled.

I was very disappointed. But I was soon compensated personally. The material that I had gathered was easily transformed into a manuscript for a book. I mentioned the incident to the late Raja

Rameshwar Rao, chairman of the publishing firm Orient Longmans (now Orient Blackswan). He took the manuscript and published it as *Hyderabad: Memoirs of a City* in 1994.

My love's labour was not lost.

* * *

Full Husband

The government's annual civil list has three categories of officers. The first comprises names of serving officers with particulars about them like age, seniority and salary. The second category is titled 'Casualties'. It names those who died in harness during the preceding year. The last category consists of the names of those who retired in the normal course. It is titled 'Wastages'. It is an ironic epitaph to those who gave their best years to public service.

I was placed on that scrap heap in 1992.

Having trudged in small steps to the highest peak of emoluments, perks and prestige, understandably employees dread the sudden fall into limbo which retirement implies.

Officers in active service dub their retired colleagues as old fogies with antiquarian notions. However, when they themselves join their ranks, they proclaim their valuable experience which should not be allowed to go waste!

Employees therefore go to any length to avoid the doom of superannuation. They fall at the feet of the chief minister; they canvass support from politicians or other influential persons who might know the chief minister. They contact the godmen known to be close to the boss. If not extension, they ask for some other job which will secure their emoluments and other perks of office.

For wives, working spouses mean half husband and full salary. They prefer that to full husband and half salary. Retired men become a nuisance at home with constant nitpicking even in domestic chores which were beneath their contempt earlier.

The point is that we prepare ourselves for twenty years for jobs which may last about thirty-five years. We are, however, entirely unprepared for post-retirement life whose span may be as long if not longer, given the progressive increase in the expectancy of life.

A Revolution

It was as if the brave new world of technology was waiting for my retirement to burst forth with all its magic.

Settling into my retirement was like waking up in a different age. Till 1990 there were only two brands of cars made in India – Ambassador and Fiat. It took sixteen years to get a car unless you were an MP or senior government officer in which case the allotment happened once in two years. We used to sell our secondhand cars at a premium. Telephony was a government monopoly. All phones were rotary and black in colour. There was a waiting period of ten years for getting a phone connection. The average period for a trunk call to a foreign country to mature took two to three days. When the complaint about the malfunctioning of the system was raised in the Lok Sabha, the then Union minister for communications, Stephen, replied arrogantly that those who were not happy with the phones could always surrender them!

In 1984 a photocopying machine was installed in the chief minister's office in Hyderabad. It was placed in the custody of his secretary who decided on every request for photocopying documents.

A year before my retirement a desktop computer was placed on my table. My P.A. did not know how to use it and so could not teach me anything about it. It needed a brief training for its use and there was a shortage of trainers. The computer could be installed only in air-conditioned rooms. We had to remove our shoes before entering the temple of computerji. The Opposition made fun of Rajiv Gandhi's advocacy of computers and warned that it would lead to unemployment. The desktop sat as a dumb status symbol in the office of every minister and secretary all over the country. Very few knew about the magical power of the computer to change our entire life.

Nobody could go abroad without a clearance of the Reserve Bank of India. The foreign exchange allowance allowed to lucky ones was US$ 500. Close relatives and friends made special requests to persons going abroad to bring a transistor radio or a wristwatch for them. Heavy custom duties were imposed on the import of all consumer goods. Returning Indians had to submit themselves to humiliating baggage and body search by custom officers.

In India economic liberalization and globalization was inaugurated in 1991. It was as if we emerged suddenly from darkness into light, from bondage into freedom, from scarcity into abundance. Imported goods became locally available. New models of cars began plying on Indian roads. Markets were flooded with fancy goods including a maddening variety of electronic gadgetry. The long-suffering consumer had finally become the king celebrated hitherto only in textbooks of economics.

A building boom ensued. Multinationals started setting up their shops in the new suburb of Hyderabad christened Cyberabad by Chandrababu Naidu.

Job Offers

From the very next day after my retirement I started receiving attractive job offers from some corporates. I knew well that they sought not my 'valuable experience', but the influence I could exert on my former juniors. I could not imagine myself as a door-opener for business honchos.

The government also offered me the job of commissioner of inquiries. I find nothing more disgusting than conducting inquiries because officials involved in them tell lies and are interested in prolonging the proceedings.

I did not want to be judged by men of straw any longer. I wanted to be in charge of my happiness. I did not want to die with an unfulfilled longing – to write.

I had made up my mind not to accept any job offer. The pension I got was reasonable considering our modest needs. I did not want to have something to *kill* time; I wanted to live it.

Of all the decisions I took in my life, that was the best.

*

Before I put the lid on my official career, I would like to say that, on the whole, I enjoyed working with my ministers. I believe that – hold your breath for the heresy – politics is the noblest profession. Yes, it is so because only through politics can you acquire the means to do maximum good for the people. We have seen that persons who want to do social service through NGOs or directly, sooner or later end up joining politics.

I hear a caveat: power corrupts. No, what Lord Acton said was that power *tends* to corrupt. That leaves a scope for hope. The unmentioned aspect of power is that power *ennobles*. The realization that you have acquired the power to translate the dreams that you dreamt for changing the world after your heart's desire is sublimating. Also, between the assumption of power and the onset of corruption there is a crucial positive interlude. In the well-known biography of Napoleon by Emile Ludwig the centerpiece carries a quotation by Goethe:

'Napoleon went forth to seek Virtue; but since she was not to be had, he got Power.'

In its true sense, politics is the pursuit of Virtue. Its lapse into 'corruption' is checked by the mechanism of periodic elections. Maybe I am too optimistic – or even naive.

A Paean to Politicians

I saw many politicians of the first generation who were genuinely interested in serving society. Many of them could not articulate their views and that is where the civil service came in. Next to politicians, the elite civil servant class has the best scope to contribute to public welfare. They help politicians to formulate policies and then proceed to implement them. Because of their background and easy accessibility to the public at large, politicians acquire a feel for the problems of the people and their mood. The best of civil servants cannot know as well as an ordinary politician where the shoe pinches.

...And Civil Servants

Here I am tempted to pay my tribute to the Indian Administrative Service, which has claimed the best years of my life. People go by its immense power and authority that imparts a just glamour to it. However, its primary attraction for the brightest and the best amongst the youth is its vast and varied scope for rendering significant service to people even at junior levels. Their training in rural India broadens the mental horizons of callow youth and introduces them to the hard realities of life in the countryside. It gives them unmatched experience at grassroots level which remains a frame of reference for the rest of their service. Even as they rise up the bureaucratic ladder they are able to relate high policy to the lives of remote humble people for whose welfare it is presumably drafted. This is made possible by the system of regular rotation between the Centre and states. The oft-repeated jibe that IAS officers are birds of passage is indeed their prime virtue. That prevents their becoming stale in any subject. By spending short spells of two to three years in various departments, they retain their objectivity and, in course of time, develop an overarching view of issues at stake. That enables them to change some of the set patterns. For the depth of an expert, they have the breadth of outlook of the generalist. In spite of frequent criticism from various quarters, most political leaders turn to IAS officers for all crucial jobs. To work with ministers with mutual respect is an enjoyable experience. I hardly ever was pressurised by any minister for doing something undesirable. In the few cases that I did, I refused without getting into any scrape except once. I must however concede that there are black sheep too and we occasionally have to hang our heads in shame that they are from our stock.

In a lighter vein, let me say that IAS is not a service. It is perpetual training. When the IAS officer completes his training in diverse fields, he is retired. All the knowledge and skills that he has acquired are for utilization in his next life. That leaves ample scope for making mistakes in this life!

***

A Second Career

My post-retirement life has been devoted largely to writing. Before I talk about that, let me make a small digression.

When I came to Hyderabad in 1959, Banjara Hills was largely uninhabited. There were no more than a dozen houses in all. A group of officers invited me to join them to buy some land for housing. The land cost less than that of long cloth – half-a-rupee per square yard! I was a believer in the Platonic injunction that the ruling class should not own private property. (He even forbade private family!) Marx was following Plato when he banished private property from his communist Utopia.

So I declined the offer.

However, I noticed that some of my colleagues known for their pronounced Marxist leanings were buying land and building houses. One of them clarified to me that building one house for self-occupation was kosher. By the time I came to my 'senses', land prices had shot up. I was then persuaded to join some friends in buying a plot in a layout of eight plots. In 1975 I paid twenty-two times the price at which I had been offered a plot earlier.

*

I moved into my house a year before my retirement. By that time all loans taken from the government had been cleared. The house was built around a massive 2.5 billion-year-old gneissic rock. All other smaller rocks in the compound were left undisturbed. In that I was inspired by the example of Nawab Mehdi Nawaz Jung who was the first to incorporate rocks in the architectural plan of the house in 1930. We built a semicircular deck facing southeast. Sitting there I could see right in front of me the iconic Charminar through the occasional haze. On my right I could see a corner of Golkonda Fort, and on my left the Venkateswara Temple atop Naubat Pahad.

After an early morning walk, I used to sit there and do my writing till my breakfast which was served to me there at eight am. In course of time the panorama from my deck was blocked as buildings kept on coming up on all sides. Finally, the western side cut off the evening sun when an eight-storey complex came up when only three storeys were permitted in Banjara Hills on a plot originally intended for one house. Famous Urdu poet and lyricist Javed Akhtar aptly described my plight in his charming couplet: 'My house has been surrounded by tall buildings / Some people have eaten up my share of the Sun.'

Later, a 'popular' chief minister modified the master plan and relaxed building rules to allow construction of multi-storey buildings in Banjara Hills. The next step down the hill was to include Banjara Hills and Jubilee Hills in the commercial category. The once 'posh' localities were thus reduced to congested, noisy habitations no different from the rest of the city. The only saving grace was that our house was in an enclave off the main road.

We produce excellent urban planning documents in India. Where we fail is in their firm implementation.

*

I had kept my childhood hobby of writing alive throughout my service. While still in service, I had published four books in Urdu and had sat on the high table of humour winning seven awards from different official literary academies in the country.

The World Humour Conference held in 1985 was an expression of my commitment to humour. I also produced a documentary in Hindi entitled *Janwar ki Pehchan* which was telecast by Doordarshan Hyderabad. Thereafter, UGC asked me to do a two-part documentary titled 'ABC of Humour'.

Finding Time

I was often asked how I found time for writing. It is strange that if an officer plays tennis or golf or cricket, and spends all his evenings in the club drinking and playing cards, nobody asks any questions. However, if one writes even one literary piece, people wonder how he found time for that. I am not a club bird, nor do I play any game. Even complimentary passes for test cricket matches could not tempt me to watch a cricket match. It was the same time – early mornings or late evenings that I devoted to my hobby. If anyone, it was my wife who was entitled to ask such a question, because I liberally stole from the time that legitimately belonged to her.

After coming to Hyderabad, for a long time Urdu dominated my writing. By the time of my retirement, I had slid into English. The readership in Urdu was shrinking fast. It had also become touchy for many topics.

I was also making a modest income from writing articles and book reviews. It grew with time and I started receiving invitations from periodicals and magazines for articles particularly relating to Hyderabad. Very soon, I was writing three columns. My 'middles' were published in all leading papers. They taught me the importance of brevity, and the computer made it possible to achieve it through its word count facility. Earlier, radio broadcasting had taught me the value of time limit and punctuality. Only at radio stations and TV studios, you see how long thirty seconds can be.

The renowned freedom fighter and journalist Yudhvir and his wife Seeta were our family friends. Yudhvir passed away in 1991. Before her death in January 1994, Seeta asked me to treat her son Vinay Vir as my own. More than my doing so, Vinay Vir and his wife Vipma have always given me the regard due to a father.

One day Vinay gave me a pleasant surprise by leaving a desktop computer as birthday gift for me to await my return from Delhi. By doing so, he also became my mentor in *computeracy*, and my computer maintenance engineer. I enjoyed using this wonderful 'toy' as Vinay called it. I hired a college dropout called Imtiaz to work for me in the forenoon. Computer is the second most user-friendly equipment made available to man! I bought a Dictaphone and dictated whatever matter I wanted to transcribe on to the computer by Imtiaz. The Dictaphone gave me flexibility in terms of working hours. I could dictate any time. I could also leave instructions for him if I was going out for any engagement. My personal target was to write 500 words per day and by and large I was able to keep it. I have till date not stopped marvelling at the versatility of the computer. The more it shrinks in size and weight, the more tasks it can accomplish. All my writings including all except the first book were done on the computer. What a saving of time and paper!

After Imtiaz left for America, I tried many young men as his replacement but found no one good enough except one. He too was lured away by a BPO. I could not match that salary. After that, I decided to be on my own with occasional help from here and there. Now that help – and guidance – comes from my two grandchildren.

In 1997 Zee Films offered me a contract for a film script in Hindi and English on the love story of Mohammad Quli Qutb Shah and Bhagmati.

That was followed by a commission for a bilingual ballet on the same subject. That was enacted in Washington.

I was frequently invited to deliver lectures at various universities and other organizations. I was also a regular on the radio and occasionally on TV. I was surprised that people still listened to radio.

In 1990 I was invited to do a monthly column for a new monthly magazine called *Channel 6*. I did that for over five years and thus was able to build up a good mass of articles on Hyderabad which came in handy on many occasions.

The *Hindu* daily had a popular weekly regional column titled 'Between You and Me'. I was requested to do that column in September 1999. I enjoyed doing that for five years after which the column was abolished nationwide. The column brought me a loyal readership and a weekly cheque.

Later *The Times of India* asked me to do a weekly column for their metro edition. It went on for about two years. When I noticed some uncalled for tampering with historical facts under the rubric of editorial privilege, I withdrew from it. For a long time, I also reviewed books for the *Deccan Chronicle* and some other papers.

Column vs Book

After a few years, I began to feel that column writing was an enemy of long-term writing. As soon as I had mailed the week's column, I would start thinking about the next week. Book reviewing, though more remunerative – considering that you get a free book in addition to cash – is even worse. You have to suffer to read books which don't even smell good. Both these exercises interfered with the discipline required for writing books. Columns, however good, have a butterfly existence; books stay longer and roam about far and wide. I therefore decided to stop doing columns and book reviews.

It was another good decision that I took.

Once I was invited to speak on Hyderabad to delegates of an international conference. I did that through a PowerPoint presentation. That led to such a recurrent demand for that show that I developed a standard show and named it 'The Romance of Hyderabad'. I kept on refining it from time to time and adapting it for specific occasions. It has been shown more than 200 times at various functions. It was also used for some inaugural and keynote addresses including the public lecture at the mid-year meeting during the platinum jubilee year of the Indian Academy of Sciences held at Hyderabad on 2 July 2009. It was also adapted for the inaugural lecture for the Hyderabad Historical Society and some other important events.

In 1985 the Cuttack Sahajoga Samiti first serialized in a magazine and then published in a book form translation of my selected writings in Urdu into Oriya and invited me to Cuttack for its release. There in a public function it conferred the title of 'Ocean of Humour' on me. I have never flaunted this unsolicited honour lest it should cause a deluge.

My humorous travelogue to America in Urdu, *Hawai Columbus*, was translated into Telugu and published in 1995 and again in 2006.

The biography of the founder of Hyderabad, mentioned earlier, was translated into Telugu by the Potti Sreeramulu Telugu University and into Urdu by the Publications Division.

When *The Memoirs of a City* went out of print, the Oxford University Press took it on and published it as *Hyderabad – A Biography* in 2006. It was translated into Telugu in 2012 by Emesco Books. A Hindi version is expected shortly.

In 1999 I produced 'Rockumentary', a documentary on the rocks of Hyderabad with a young man, Mohammad Ali Baig. Within weeks of its production it won two international awards at the Japan International Heritage Films Festival held in Kyoto in 1999. It was also telecast by Doordarshan.

The Society to Save Rocks won a national award for the best NGO in tourism in 2003. The same year I wrote a slim volume on the subject at the request of the tourism department of Andhra Pradesh. In 2012 it was published as a coffee-table book titled *The Rockscape of Andhra Pradesh*.

*

The great pioneering photographer of India, Raja Deen Dayal, had earned his glory during the twenty years of his stay in Hyderabad beginning in 1885. I was keen on establishing a museum of photography to commemorate him. I believed that the museum would find international support and would soon grow into a university of 'imageology'. I was able to persuade the chief minister, N.T. Rama Rao, to sanction two million rupees for the project. However, the project did not fructify due to lack of necessary support from Deen Dayal's descendants. I therefore surrendered the grant and got down to researching Deen Dayal on my own. I visited his ancestral town Sardhana in Meerut district of Uttar Pradesh and was surprised to know that no one there had heard his name. The Roorkee Engineering College where Deen Dayal had done a diploma in draughtsmanship had full record about his education. The college became an IIT in 2005.

My friend, late Dr K. Anji Reddy, the pioneering founder of Dr Reddy's Labs, offered to sponsor a book on Raja Deen Dayal.

Sandhya's small publishing outfit Creative Point published the book *Raja Deen Dayal – Prince of Photographers* in 2003. The Prince of Wales wrote a foreword for it.

My book served to correct some myths and factual mistakes about Deen Dayal. Hitherto it was said that he had excelled in photography which he studied in the college. Further, it was routinely stated that he died in 1910. In fact, there was no course in photography in the college. He cultivated it as a hobby. Nor did he top in his class. Lastly, he passed away in 1905. That meant that a lot of photographs which had passed off as his were not taken by him. Two post-doctoral scholars from the US told me that they had to make corrections in their theses after going through my book.

Hitherto most books on Deen Dayal had said that he had learnt photography in the college and had stood first in his class. My research showed that none of these was correct.

I was later commissioned by Doordarshan to do a documentary on Raja Deen Dayal. I visited the places associated with Deen Dayal again with a crew. Based on my further research for the documentary, a second edition of the book on Deen Dayal was published by 'Hyderabad.in' in 2006. The few copies now available have become collector's items.

In the course of research on Hyderabad, I had read an Urdu book by an Urdu poet who was attached to the Junior Prince of Hyderabad for seven years beginning in 1931. The prince used to stay awake at night and sleep off during the day. I found it very interesting and purely for fun translated it into English. The Oxford University Press published it as *The Nocturnal Court*.

In 2013 I was introduced to a new publisher. Niyogi Books published *Legendotes of Hyderabad* in 2014. A new edition is in the works.

Research vs Creativity

Fairly early on I began to realize that research was an enemy of creative writing. Before getting sucked into the swamp of research, I could produce a story or an article in one sitting anywhere. Now I could not write without extensively researching the subject. I mourned the loss of my felicity in creative writing. And then I happened upon the case of William Morris, the nineteenth-century artist, painter, poet, textile designer – in short, a versatile artist. In 1877 he was invited to accept the chair of poetry at the Oxford University. His classic reply declining the offer is framed and hangs in the library of Exeter College, Oxford. In that he says that '...the practice of any art rather narrows the artist in regard to the theory of it...' My case was the mirror image of that phenomenon. But unlike him I did not foresee the consequences of my gradual slide into research. I often regret the shift but it is too late for me to return home to creativity.

On Writing and Inspiration

On my retirement, I prepared a list of ten books which I wished to write. As a daily self-reminder I pinned the list on the soft board in front of my desk in my study. In the years since then, I have overshot my target. This is my fourteenth book in English. Every book and documentary has a story.

I have another quote on the board in front of me which stares me in the face every time I come to my desk. It reads:

'The art of writing is the art of applying the seat of the pants to the seat of the chair'

Mary Heaton Vorse (b. 1894)

It is very true. Although there are productive and barren phases in life, there is no question of 'mood'. I create mood as a part of my daily drill.

Recently, I came across another insightful saying by the American author, publisher and parachute designer, Don Poynter: 'If you wait for inspiration to arrive, you are a waiter, not a writer.'

There is no dearth of topics to write on. On the contrary, I feel one with the famous Urdu poet Sauda who said:

Kehtaa hai yehi khaamaa keh kis kis ko main baandhoon
Baadal se chale aate hain mazmoon mere aage
(My pen wonders what topic it should choose
They come in hordes like clouds in the sky)

The other important point is revision. I have quoted Galbraith earlier. I was gratified to read in his autobiography[10] that whatever he wrote, he revised and wrote four or five times. I do the same – notice permitting.

Galbraith also admitted that he was poor in the use of the article. His secretary used to do the necessary corrections. I was heartened to know that I shared my weakness with someone whom I admire. However, that is not to say that I am anywhere near him in his limpid prose.

When I am writing, I am enjoying. Every word, every sentence, every page is a building block for a final edifice. T.S. Eliot speaks for me when he says:

[10] J.K. Galbraith, A *Life in Our Times: Memoirs*

...Consequently I rejoice,
Having to construct something
Upon which to rejoice...[11]

*

Apart from writing, some unsolicited and interesting consultancy assignments came my way from BBC, Arthur Anderson, Ernst and Young, and others.

I also served on boards of some companies after my retirement for some time. The ease with which the private sector plays with public funds frightened me. I was lucky that I got out without getting into any scrape.

* * *

[11] T.S. Eliot, 'Ash Wednesday'. I don't know how the experts would interpret this poem. This is my understanding of the stanza

A Sick Family

One day Sandhya rang up from Delhi to suggest a rehabilitation home at Mumbai called 'Kripa' for Rahul.

I lost no time in taking Rahul there.

The rehab was depressing. The director of the rehab was of big build and wore a hardened look. It did not exude any empathy for me. I did not know then that he was himself a former addict. Most rehabs are run by former addicts who know the tricks of the trade.

He explained to me the nature of addiction and the line of the 'treatment'. And then suddenly blurted out: 'You are a sick family.'

'How?'

'Because Rahul is running after the bottle and all of you are running after him to keep him away from the bottle.'

'So?'

'So, all of you are suffering from one obsession. *That* is your sickness.'

I had not yet fully absorbed the impact of his remark when he added, 'You and your wife are the *enablers* for Rahul. You are supporting him financially thus making it possible for him to continue his addiction. You are therefore responsible for his condition – and your plight.'

'If we don't do that, how will he manage?'

'Let him realize that.'

His explanation drove the point home. My hope soared.

'What should we do then?' I asked like a defeated soldier laying down his arms.

'Throw him out of the house.'

The father in me was alarmed at this suggestion. 'He might then die.'

'Only when he sees death in front of him, will he get the motivation to try to kick the addiction.'

For the first time his face became mobile.

'QED,' struck by the insight, I murmured to myself.

I told the director that Rahul had steel rods in his legs and so could not squat. Thereupon he directed me to a shop nearby from where I could buy a commode. Finding no help, I carried it all the way to the rehab. I was amused at my plight but felt grateful that no one recognized me there.

Rahul did not like the place. The director took me aside and advised me to slip away quietly while he engaged him in conversation.

I returned home with a feeling of peace and a glimmer of hope that Rahul would soon come home a changed man. However, barely had a fortnight passed when the director of Kripa rang me up to say that they could not keep Rahul there any longer. He was spoiling the discipline of the institution. I pleaded with him to try to make another attempt.

A week later he rang up again and said that if I did not take him away, he would discharge him and would not be responsible for the consequences.

He added that I had the option of washing my hands off Rahul and leave him to own devices in Mumbai. 'Here he might resort to begging or commit some crime to survive. Mafia dons look for that sort of person. He might then end up in jail or even die on the roadside. It would be better therefore to get him a train ticket for Hyderabad, give him another 200 rupees and tell him that henceforth he was on his own. Only then will he agree to submit to treatment.'

I went to Mumbai and got Rahul discharged. He was full of resentment against us and the rehab.

At the Mumbai State Guest House where I was staying, I handed Rahul his ticket and then adding another 200 rupees, told him that he would not be allowed to enter my house. Stunned by my declaration, he asked, 'Then where should I go?'

'Anywhere,' I don't know how I brought myself to say that. 'I don't care. But you will not enter my house.' I was choking when I uttered those heartless words. I rushed to the washroom to wipe my tears and wash my face. By the time I returned a few minutes later, Rahul was nowhere to be seen. Our plan was that I would put him in the train and see him off. I panicked finding him nowhere. The guest house staff told me that they had seen a man on crutches catch a bus. He would not have known which bus would take him to the station. I asked my driver to rush me to the railway station. There I saw Rahul from a distance getting into the train. I was relieved. Now he would reach Hyderabad safely.

We learnt that Rahul had gone to one of his old addict friends. We did not like that but then we were supposed not to care. His friend fed us with lies. Once he reported that Rahul had gone to a hotel close by and incurred a heavy bill for drinking. We quietly paid the amount he mentioned. Soon it became a racket and I had to tell him that we would not bail him out in the future.

Thereupon he showed Rahul the door. For some time, we did not know where he was but news about him would come from some source or the other.

Part of that time he was in Bengaluru. For some time, he stayed with Bindi's cousin Raman and her husband Trilok Gulati. After a month or so Trilok moved Rahul to the guest room in his factory. Trilok never mentioned to us how he coped with him. But we remember him and Raman with gratitude.

The Royal Astrologer

Our neighbour and old college fellow Vijay Katoch is a nephew of the late Maharaja of Jammu and Kashmir. The royal astrologer of Jammu and Kashmir used to visit him once a year for a few days. Whenever he came, Vijay would invite us for the special puja and the lunch thereafter. Once he told Bindi that she could ask the astrologer anything she wanted to. This was a special favour because normally the astrologer confined himself only to matters concerning the members of Kashmir's royal family. Even before Bindi opened her mouth, the astrologer surprised us by telling her that she was worried about two issues – Sandhya's marriage and Rahul's addiction. About Sandhya, he said that she had a woman's body but a man's spirit in her and we need not worry about her. 'She is a person of solid character and a loner in life. She has no deep attachments.' He added that she might marry about two years hence. If she did not, she would become a spiritual person and there was even a likelihood of her renunciation of the material world.

About Rahul, he said that he would become alright when his daughter attained the age of eight. There was a possibility of his reunion with his wife Rajeshwari in 1997. After that, there would be a very successful period for him for thirty-five years.

The prediction about Sandhya turned out to be partially correct. She did not marry. Instead, she turned to Tibetan Buddhism and unbeknownst to us even became a practising Buddhist. She started devouring every available book on Buddhism and meditation, and began attending teachings by every Buddhist teacher who happened to be in or passing through Delhi. She also met the Dalai Lama a few times. She often visited Dharamsala to attend initiations and teachings there. In this way, she began to cultivate her spiritual life while she supported herself financially with her consultancy work. In 1999 she got a fellowship for studying advanced Buddhism at the Naropa University in Boulder, Colorado. It is a unique institute founded by a renowned Tibetan teacher, who wanted to bring together the wisdom traditions of the East with the liberal arts tradition of the West to devise a programme that offered 'contemplative education'. The students were also required to do regular meditation. She completed a three-year degree and became one of the first to obtain a Masters of Divinity degree in Buddhism. Soon after, she was appointed as assistant dean in the same university.

Thereafter Sandhya decided to top off her experience in communication with an MA in International and Intercultural Communication from the University of Denver. After completing that, she served as director of advocacy of a statewide Anti-Violence Programme in Denver, where she oversaw services to survivors of violence. Alongside, she continued with her study of Buddhism, using whatever breaks she got from her work to go for meditation retreats. Her training as a Buddhist chaplain entitles her to teach meditation practices.

She also pursued her passion for photography. She held an exhibition of her photos in Boulder in 2013.

The prediction about Rahul meant that there was hope for us about three years hence.

***

AB MAIN NACHYON BAHUT, GOPALA

Our bedevilment with Rahul's addiction continued unabated. In mid 1996 Sandhya again suggested that we send Rahul to 'Freedom Foundation' in Bengaluru.

I was advised that we put Rahul in an overnight bus and they would pick him up next morning.

We sent our trusted servant Sunder to escort Rahul to the bus station. When I rang up Freedom Foundation the next morning, they said that he had not come. After some time, I got a call from a lodge in Hyderabad that Rahul was there and that he did not have money to clear his bills. What had happened was that after reaching the bus station and after Sunder had handed him his ticket, Rahul told him to go away. He would be able to manage on his own. As soon as Sunder turned his back, Rahul got down from the bus, sold his ticket to a person who was on the waiting list, got into a nearby lodge and started drinking. I had to pay a hefty bill to the lodge to get him out. Next evening, I myself drove Rahul to the bus stop, put him in the bus and waited till the bus had started.

Rahul stayed in the rehab for six months. After about a month, I was asked to go there for a 'confrontation' with Rahul. This is done to make the client face the complaints that the family had against him.

The facility was located in an open place outside the city from where the inmates could escape if they liked. The philosophy of the Freedom Foundation was that they would not keep a client against his will.

To my surprise, Rahul listened to me without rebutting any charge. The 'confrontation' went off pretty well. A month later they asked both Bindi and me to come for another, broader 'confrontation'. We had to share the common meal of rice, dal and curd served in old battered aluminium plates. It was like an ashram but with a dismal air hanging over it. However, we were pleasantly surprised that Rahul did not complain about the conditions there. In fact, he seemed to take some pride in narrating the daily routine to us and made light of the hardship involved. That 'confrontation' also went off well. We recited a litany of his misdemeanours to the counsellor at Rahul's face, and again he did not rebut any of them. This transformation in his behaviour gave us hope.

Rajeshwari and Raisa also had to go to Bengaluru for interaction with Rahul as a part of his therapy. Though divorced, Rahul and Rajeshwari were in touch.

At the end of the prescribed period, Rahul came home a changed person and we were overjoyed with the result. But, alas! It did not last long. One day Rahul came home drunk. Seeing him in that state, all our hopes collapsed. The only redeeming feature was that next day he himself said he would go back to the rehab for another spell.

Meanwhile Rajeshwari had left her job in 1994. She had good postgraduate qualifications and so started on her own as a consultant. It was rather stressful for her and so I spoke to my friend Kishen Chugh, then chairman of I.T.C. Thanks to him, Rajeshwari was appointed in the Human Resource Division of VST Industries. It was a job with regular working hours and a good salary. She was a good worker and was liked by her colleagues and superiors. She had quick grasp and learnt the ropes very fast. Meanwhile her parents had moved to Mehdipatnam, not far from our house, and she and Raisa started spending weekends with us.

In 1999 VST set up a new factory at Zaheerabad and Rajeshwari was posted there. She could not shift there and commuting to the factory there took about four hours by the company car. She had to leave home before Raisa got up in the morning. By the time she returned Raisa would already be asleep. That did not suit her and so in January 2000 she resigned and joined an IT company as manager.

Rahul went back to Freedom Foundation once more in 1998. He now seemed to be sufficiently motivated to get rid of his addiction.

However, repeated relapses had broken our back. We could see no light at the end of the tunnel. We were getting old and Rahul's problem seemed to be unending. There was no knowing how long I would survive.

We were fatigued in life's journey only on that count. I felt like Surdas who, after a life of complete devotion of singing and dancing before his deity Krishna, finally decided to give up. Frustrated, he uttered his final wail – *Ab main nachyon bahut, Gopala!* (I have danced enough, O Krishna!)[12] At that epiphanous moment, it is said, the statue of Krishna in front of him came alive and played his flute for Surdas.

When would the flute play for us?

---

[12] Surdas was a blind saint, Hindi poet and musician of Braj near Mathura in the fifteenth-sixteenth centuries. He is known for his devotional songs dedicated to Lord Krishna. He used to dance in ecstasy before the statue of his deity

Rahul finished his spell at Freedom Foundation in Bengaluru and returned to Hyderabad in 2001.

Soon after that, he did a course in Vipassana meditation for a week. At the end of the course, to our surprise, Rahul said that he would like to stay longer at the rehab in Bengaluru. He stayed there for a year. He was made a counsellor in the rehab which meant that we did not have to pay for his keep. It was also supposed to be good for his recovery. Later, he was encouraged to pick up a job in an advertising company but continued to stay in the Freedom Foundation campus. It was as if he was learning step-by-step to integrate with the real world from which his addiction had cut him off.

Before his discharge, I was asked to visit the Foundation and meet with his counsellor and his sponsor, named Krishna. In the terminology of the Alcoholics Anonymous, 'sponsor' is a senior addict who has been sober, or what they call 'clean' for a long time, say twenty years or so. It is customary for every addict to have a sponsor. He is a friend, philosopher and guide of the junior addict turned sober.

They organized an informal farewell gathering of all the clients in the evening. I was asked to speak there. After saying a few words, I broke down and wanted to cry openly. Krishna started massaging my back gently. That was soothing like balm on an aching limb. I tried to speak but again broke down. Then I muttered a few words of gratitude and brought Rahul back to Hyderabad in 1998. He had been away for two years.

At that time Freedom Foundation set up a branch at Hyderabad. Rahul was appointed as a counsellor there. Incidentally, there is nothing like having been 'cured' of alcoholism. All sober addicts call themselves 'recovering alcoholics'. They may relapse any time. All addicts live from day to day. They celebrate the day of the beginning of their sobriety as their birthday. They commonly recite the following 'Serenity Prayer' before dinner:

> *God, grant me the serenity to accept the things I cannot change; courage to change the things I can; and wisdom to know the difference.*

AA meetings are held at some church, a denominational school, or even the residence of the archbishop.

The AA credo has a God but it can be God of any faith. I was brought up in the liberal Hindu tradition. By my youth I had outgrown that and become an atheist under the influence of J.S. Mill. In Rahul's childhood, I had told him what Mill's father had told him regarding God: 'If God made everything, who made Him?'

I was surprised to see Rahul going to a temple with Rajeshwari.

That set me thinking. Atheism is based entirely on rationalism. Logic alone can't justify the existence of God just as it can't explain so many other mysteries of life. A good deal of human life is beyond the pale of logic. An atheist stands alone in his self-confidence. Strong on reason, he is emotionally sterile. There are moments when you look for some support, some comforting hand on your cheek. Perfectly normal persons seek solace when they are defeated. God is then the default post to turn to for comfort. No belief system can stand scrutiny, yet a preponderant majority of humankind live and die for their faith.

Over the years, I mellowed into an agnostic. It is a midway position without spiritual opportunism.

*

It was around this time in early 2000 that Rajeshwari and Rahul started living together for Raisa's sake. They hired a flat next to M.F. Husain's studio not far from our house. We saw a broken marriage being repaired bit by bit and a home emerging from the four walls of a bare flat. The hymeneal glow which was missing in Delhi was visible now. We visited them every evening. We contributed some household item off and on to help flesh up the new home faster.

It was good to see the little family together and happy. Rajeshwari had a home now. She spoke with the pride of a mistress of the house. Sometimes she asked us to stay on for dinner. We felt delighted. The euphoria of an evening was a brushstroke which painted a warm soothing colour over the sooty past. Everything was forgotten, forgiven. Nothing had ever happened. We had got our son back. Was it for real? A fear always lurked at the back of our mind whenever he went out. Would he come back sober? When would he relapse? Months passed in a daze of disbelief.

Second Marriage

One day in 2001 Rahul and Rajeshwari came to us and said they wanted to get married again. 'Are you sure?' I asked, 'a second divorce won't be easy.'

In 2001, we went to the registrar. Rajeshwari's father and Rahul's counsellor, Karl, came along. After Rahul had signed in the register, the registrar asked, 'Who is the bride?'

Rajeshwari stepped up. 'The same bride!' the registrar exclaimed involuntarily and everybody burst into laughter. Bindi had brought a packet of sweets. They were distributed to all present in the hall.

Rishabh, their son, was born on 5 October 2001.

*

Our happiness was short-lived. One day Rajeshwari came home downcast and told us that Rahul had relapsed. We were struck dumb for a few moments. Then having absorbed the shock we asked her how it had happened. 'Like it always does,' she said, 'he met some old buddy of his. They drank a bit and that was the end.' 'What will happen now?' asked Bindi in panic. 'He goes down to the snake's tail as in the game of Snakes and Ladders. To the starting point,' Rajeshwari replied stoically.

Rahul had to leave the job and went back to Bengaluru to do another spell. It had been close to thirty years since the beginning of our misery and yet there did not seem to be any closure in sight. There were false starts and glimmers of hope but what was constant was defeat at every turn. What we had seen in the last few months was a mirage. There was no promised land in sight. We had to continue walking in the vast unending desert, very likely to the end of our blighted lives.

I tried to close my eyes to what was happening all around. I diverted my attention by busying myself in various ways, mostly by writing, but the nagging pain of Rahul's addiction intruded stealthily demanding attention. It superseded everything. Wherever we were, our thoughts about Rahul followed us like a shadow. But no, shadows fall outside of us. This shadow fell inside us. It penetrated whatever armour we wore; it scalded the place it fell upon. And how many such shadows had we absorbed? In public we stood erect, we smiled, we entertained, did everything which normal humans do. Our hurt was deep, a private curse we carried within us wherever we went. We were weary with the load but there was no place we could put it down. 'Hope is the thing with feathers,' the poet Emily Dickinson had aptly said. With us it had lost all its feathers.

Patanjali in his *Yoga Sutra* says that the nature of mind is to wander. Yoga is to control that nature of the mind and to bring it to concentrate at one point. In a curious way, we were able to do that. Our minds kept on coming back to one point – Rahul.

***

'WITH FEATHERS'

On return from 'Freedom', in January 2001, Rahul started working with an NGO involved with HIV.

After about six months one day Rajeshwari and Rahul came together to our house. He had lately been talking of setting up a rehab of his own. It was to be better than the ones which he had stayed in and seen. 'Upmarket,' he said with his old flair. Was he back to his old grandiosity, I wondered.

'So...' I waited for elaboration.

'I need an investment of two lakhs,' he said.

I recalled the time twenty years ago in Delhi when he wanted to set up a rabbit farm near Nainital. Some friend of his had sold the idea to him. 'Investment of one lakh rupees only. Quick returns, the way the rabbits breed,' he had said excitedly.

'Have you prepared a project report?' I had asked.

'You and your project reports,' Rahul had growled and stomped out of the room.

I feared a repeat of the same scene.

Instead, he produced sheets of papers from his pocket and, putting them on the table, started to explain the figures to me. They seemed to make sense. I asked Rajeshwari if she supported the proposal. Earlier, that would have been an excuse for him to kick up a shindy. He kept quiet. She said she agreed with him.

I got up and wrote a cheque for the amount. 'A loan,' I said, 'payable when…' and muttered as in a soliloquy, 'and if able.'

After Rahul and Rajeshwari left, I told Bindi, 'Our last gamble.' Mentally, I wrote off the amount. In the best of cases, the project would take a year to break even.

'Hope Trust' was started on 10 August 2002. It broke even in three months. Clients came. The year ended with a surplus. 'Hope' *had* feathers, after all!

For long accustomed to living in a state of constant fear, we waited for the dreaded word – 'relapse'. Bindi and I worried separately – and together. Weeks passed, then months, then a year – and more. Our suspense and fear persisted. Dreams can't last that long. One day after two years, Rahul and Rajeshwari came together to see us. We sat down around our circular dining table. Rahul smiled and proffered an envelope to me. I opened the cover. It had a cheque for rupees two lakhs. Rahul said he was returning the loan he had taken. In disbelief I said there was no hurry. He smiled and said the loan should be repaid – the sooner the better. Since then many more years have passed. We kept our fingers crossed. 'Will it last? And for how long?' Worry, as Saint Kabir had said, is a robber who gnaws at your heart; no physician has any cure for that.[13] We had to learn to come out of that deep dark well of worry to enjoy our new-found deliverance. It had been a long, arduous journey. But we had made it.

*

[13] Kabir was a fifteenth-century mystic, poet and saint born in Varanasi. The full doha is: *'Chinta aisi daakini kaat kalejaa khaae / Baid becharaa kyaa kare kab tak kare dwaai'*

The nub of drug abuse (alcohol is also a drug) is that it is an illness, not a moral issue. In the words of Bill W., co-founder of AA,[14] the addict is 'sick but not sinful'. It is therefore unfair and pointless to try to 'reform' the addicts. To try to invoke their will power is also no use. They are simply helpless before the drug. What compounds the situation is that addicts are also allergic to the object of their obsession.

There is no medical 'treatment' for the disease of drug abuse. In fact, some physicians themselves fall prey to drug addiction. No medicine is given for 'curing' the patient of the addiction. Before the revolution in understanding the nature of addiction and the way to handle it was brought about by Bill Wilson and Dr Bob Smith in 1935, physicians in America used to give addicts castor oil and belladonna. They did not do any good. Carl Jung, one of the pioneers of modern psychology, in a letter to Bill W. in 1961 agreed that 'the only answer for an alcoholic was some sort of change of heart'. The treatment therefore aims to bring about 'a spiritual wakening' and a corresponding change in thinking and lifestyle of the addict. It follows that the best persons to treat addicts are not qualified medical men but ex-addicts or, as they prefer to call themselves, 'recovering addicts'. The counsellors in rehab centres are generally such people. In the course of 'treatment', the client is made to go over his past, acknowledge the damage he has done to himself and others, to make a moral inventory of self, and to make amends to those whom he has wronged. Interventions are arranged at proper intervals with the immediate members of the family including parents, spouse and children who narrate their hurts in the presence of other clients

[14] Alcoholics Anonymous (AA) is an international mutual aid fellowship founded in 1935 by Bill Wilson and Dr Bob Smith in Akron, Ohio

and counsellors. The treatment thus is an experience of a spiritual change, akin to a religious conversion without the involvement of any religion in the conventional sense of the term.

All this we learnt during the course of Rahul's addiction – and later. Whenever we have narrated our story to others, many of them have come out of their own denial and often embarked on a journey of recovery. I write this also with the same hope. There is no shame or guilt in this as there is none in any disease including diabetes or cancer. However, the anonymity of the client and the family is scrupulously maintained.

'Hope Trust' was well received. *The Reader's Digest* counted it amongst the top five in India. Rahul and Rajeshwari kept on upgrading the quality of their facilities and personal care. They started getting clients from abroad, from England, Canada, the United States, the Gulf, Singapore, and Thailand, and even from Russia. Some 'political' high ups came under cover of darkness and extracted a promise that their identity would not be revealed. They wanted a little extra anonymity than is in any case kept for every inmate.

The gratitude of families whose near ones are reclaimed at 'Hope' is heartwarming. Rahul and Rajeshwari have visited facilities abroad. They continue to attend fellowships of Alcoholics Anonymous all over India and abroad, including England and the US. Rajeshwari also ran some special programmes in the old city along with the City Police of Hyderabad. There was no money in that but it was a part of their outreach efforts.

*

We were keen to provide free treatment for poor addicts. Rahul applied for the scheme under the Union ministry of social welfare and justice for aid to set up a unit. After considerable follow-up with the state government, the application was recommended to the Union government. There was no response from Delhi. Then someone rang up. The anonymous male voice said if he was paid Rs 25,000 he would get the sanction letter from the ministry. I spoke to senior officers in the ministry. Nothing happened. Rahul said it was good in a way not to get involved with the government. There would be piles of forms to be filled up, delays in the release of grants, inspections and reports and unending demands for bribes. Well-intentioned schemes get embroiled in red tape and corruption.

*

The concern shown by Rahul and Rajeshwari for us in so many ways is touching. On the golden jubilee of our wedding, they secretly planned a gala evening and invited people from near and far. Somehow we got wind of it and forced them to call it off. We had never indulged in such conspicuous expenditure. But it felt good to know that we have children who cared. About fifteen years ago, they surprised me by gifting me a laptop on my birthday, as Vinay Vir had gifted me my first desktop. I was shocked. I did not believe it. I resisted such an expensive gift. They persisted and it was a pleasure finally to yield.

In 2007 when Bindi and I made a trip to China, Rahul put 1000 dollars in my pocket. I asked him if he wanted anything brought for him. He said it was for us to spend. But we did not know how to blow. Years of parsimony had rendered us unfit to indulge ourselves. We did not touch the packet and brought it back. Both husband and wife protested.

It seems now that we once had a little boy, a lovely child with lots of promise. That golden icon was stolen from us and buried under debris for thirty years. After painful searches and prolonged excavations, it was finally retrieved, scrubbed clean, polished, restored to its original shape and then returned to us. Rahul is a feeling, loving son like we had never experienced before. Whatever we need or he thinks we need, he provides unasked. Every now and then he gives us a pleasant surprise. He meets us every day either before he goes to work or on his return in the evening. We talk about small things, about his children, our grandchildren and their progress. He shares his new plans and vision for his venture. Some evenings he suddenly suggests that we go out for dinner or a movie – or both. All of us fit into his SUV easily.

We believe Rajeshwari has come into our family as a blessing. It was good that she disregarded my warning against marrying Rahul. She has virtues rarely to be found together in one person. On many occasions, in stray incidents, she has shown maturity and wisdom beyond her years. She exhibits deep understanding, infinite empathy, and patience in her relationships. She makes friends easily and builds trusting networks. She anticipates our needs like a mother and has a solution for every problem. In more than two decades of her marriage, there has been no misunderstanding with her ever on any matter. Bindi and Rajeshwari are very close to each other. She reminds me of the moving story by the renowned Urdu writer, the late Rajinder Singh Bedi, about a new bride titled '*Apne dukh mujhe de do*' (Handover your woes to me).

Her gestures to us on various occasions – and on no occasion – have always been touching. She has brought the gift of sunshine to our house. The giggles and laughter we heard in other houses now emanate from ours.

That is the sum of the happiness to which our grandchildren have contributed. Raisa is a charming woman of twenty-five. She came back home in 2014 after earning an MSc in mental health with merit from King's College London. She has a good voice and is nimble on her feet. She performed her *arangetram* in Bharatanatyam on 27 April 2014 while working at Hope. Rishabh, all of fourteen, besides being a good student, plays in a band, and is my Cortana for the computer and mobile phone.

*

I have been to Pakistan twice since we left it in 1947. In 1962 I went as a member of the Indian delegation to attend ECAFE session at Karachi which was then the capital of Pakistan. At that time our house in Dharampura and my maternal grandfather's kothi on the Infantry Road were intact. The occupant family of the latter was a Muslim refugee family from Amritsar. The members of the family were very hospitable to me and unbeknownst to me, had paid the driver of the taxi the full fare due from me for the day. I came to know of it only at the end of the day when the driver told me that I did not have to pay him anything!

In the other house at Dharampura, the occupants were the poor buffalo herders from the *basti* close to our street. Immediately after the outbreak of riots in the city they lost no time in occupying all the houses in the street. The head of the family occupying our house told me that they had found a big stock of cloth and other miscellaneous items from the big almirah in the bedroom. I told him that they were items of dowry collected piece by piece by my mother during the days of rationing. He smiled and said, 'What a surprise! We put them to the right use as dowry for our daughter's marriage!'

In 2005 Bindi and I paid a private visit to Lahore for a fortnight.

This time the landscape had changed so much. We were not able to locate our house and just arrived in time to see my grandfather's kothi under demolition for 'development'.

In Lahore, the Punjab government's department of language and culture hosted a reception in my honour. The majority of local persons in the reception were writers and poets of Urdu which is the official language of Pakistan. However, all the proceedings were conducted in Punjabi. I read some of my compositions in Urdu for the elite gathering.

Later we visited Bindi's ancestral town, Bhalwal. A high school was being run on the ground floor of her ancestral mansion at Bhalwal. She took me on the second floor and showed me the room where she was born. Then she picked up a piece of wood from the room as a keepsake. There was no trace of appurtenant orchards and the factory. The granddaughter of the personal maid of Bindi's grandmother was insistent that we have lunch with the family. We did not have time for that. She also put a sack of Mausambis called 'Fruitus' in the boot of the taxi. Her husband said proudly that the region produced so much of the fruit that it was called the 'California of Pakistan'.

From there we went to Malakwal, the house in which Bindi's parents last stayed before Partition. It was inhabited by a number of young brothers and their families. They were very excited about a visit from the 'owner's family'. The labour contractor of Bindi's family factory was an eighty-five-year-old man and he rattled off the names of Bindi's parents and uncles. Bindi used to talk about her family's riches and property. This visit confirmed that I had married an ex-rich girl!

We received a warm reception wherever we went. We were taken to the Lahore Fort. Our guide bought tickets from the counter. As we made for the entrance, the ticket clerk stopped the guide and asked him to buy foreigners' tickets for us.

It hit me suddenly. Notwithstanding all the hospitality, I was a foreigner in my own city!

*

Let me wrap up this story with my family.

My father passed away in 1972.

I was in Delhi on an official visit and as usual I had planned to visit my parents in Gurgaon in the evening. Instead, I had to visit my parents-in-law. Next morning, I flew back to Hyderabad. In the evening my father felt feverish. The family doctor advised my mother to take him to Delhi. My mother hired a taxi and reached the Ram Manohar Lohia Hospital. The doctor had a look at him, felt his pulse and said 'brought dead'. I got a phone call in the middle of the night.

In 1989, I was taken seriously ill and was sent to All India Institute of Medical Sciences (AIIMS) on the basis of a misdiagnosis in Hyderabad. When I did not return for a month, my mother flew from Hyderabad to Delhi. She told me that she had prayed to God to transfer my illness to her and spare my life – just as Mughal Emperor Babar had done for his son Humayun.

For the duration of my stay in hospital, she stayed with my youngest brother, Gogo. After my recovery, Bindi and I dropped in at his house on our way to the airport to meet my mother before leaving for Hyderabad. She had gone out for dinner to another relative's house. We therefore could not meet her. Gogo and his wife Jaishree had also gone out separately for dinner. They returned rather late at night. My mother was awake and she asked Gogo to fetch her some water. Gogo helped mother get up and resting her head against his chest, offered her the glass of water. She took a sip from the glass and said, 'OK. I am going now.'

Gogo teased her, 'Where are you going at this late hour?'

There was no reply.

I was the favourite son of my parents. Yet, I was the only one who missed seeing them just before they crossed over!

My younger brother and buddy, Vijay, was the keenest and the first to migrate to the US. He passed away due to kidney failure in 2005 aged seventy. His son Pablo sent me a ticket to join the other brothers to be able to see him three days before he died.

Vijay did not respond to my greetings. He did not utter a word before he closed his eyes.

His wife Gago is Bindi's younger sister. She and two of her sons with their families live in San Jose. Her daughter Tanya lives in New Delhi. Her two children are studying in America. They are already US citizens.

My elder brother Surendra, aged ninety-one, was in and out of American hospitals before his death in 2015. His wife had died a few years earlier. His two sons and their families are doing well in the US.

My sister Nimmi passed away in 2013 in Faridabad.

Her husband Kartar Singh had predeceased her in 1988. She left behind three sons and one daughter. All of them have children and are all doing well.

Gogo and his wife Jaishree live in New Jersey. Both their sons are married and have families and are well off.

I am the only sibling alive in India.

Now Kirpa Ram's family is left with only one male line in India.

***

MEDITATION AND MEDITATIONS

Sandhya came back to Hyderabad in mid 2014 after an absence of twenty-five years – fourteen of them were spent in the US.

As expected, she went through quite a bit of adjustment issues and some level of frustration. There were many changes that she had to condition herself to. The city had grown both in extent and density. The chaotic traffic, power breakdowns and noise levels from places of worship were constant irritations to which we had reconciled.

Fortunately, she had a good number of friends she had kept in touch with, and was able to settle in quite well socially, also making new friends.

She set up a small organization which focused on meditation and travel.

Things moved slowly for her: her idea for her work was interesting and she wanted to utilize her education and experience at Naropa University and Boulder to create courses and a space to share her passion for spiritual teachings, in particular Buddhism. Meditation is the central part of this endeavour and she gradually developed modules to reach out to diverse audiences. But the marketing effort continues to bog her down. People have a lot of curiosity and a great desire to take care of their rising stress and anxiety levels. But their interest is not often translated into a deeper resolve to explore their inner world. That exploration is usually difficult and uncomfortable. Most abandon it as soon as they find out that before they experience any kind of release they might have to do some challenging inner work.

While it has been a positive experience for her to 'come back home', she misses her quiet environment. She enjoyed living alone in the US for many years, while here she is constantly surrounded by people. She also came from a city in the US where there was a lot of open and beautiful space, right at the foothills of the Rocky Mountains and, both metaphorically and literally, she feels far more constrained in Hyderabad. She hopes to travel frequently to the mountains, where she finds much to explore in terms of the history of India's religions and spirituality.

Lately, Rajeshwari and she got into a new hobby of kitchen gardening. They set up their projects – Rajeshwari on her terrace and Sandhya on the deck of our house. She spent a good deal of time on that and we started getting supplemental supplies of salads and vegetables from our kitchen garden. There is a very good feeling when you see plants grow from day-to-day and you attend to the various problems associated with the growth of any organism. It is like children growing up before your eyes, or keeping a pet. As a young girl she always had a pet dog. Now she has outgrown that and seems to have passed on that love to her niece Raisa in redoubled measure.

Just as she did when she was younger, she continues to study – researching in her field. Every now and then she picks up her camera and indulges her interest in photography. She had a small exhibition in the US a few years ago, but hasn't shown her work here in Hyderabad.

My Meditations

Seeing Sandhya absorbed in meditation for long hours in her room, one day I asked her to teach me some meditation techniques. She explained them to me verbally and then asked me to do my own practise.

I tried to sit down some evenings when I do my physical exercises. I followed Sandhya's directions, but could not concentrate even for a moment. My monkey mind keeps hopping in all directions. Thoughts of various kinds assail my mind.

I think of the larger human family. The world stands on the edge of a precipice today. We are virtually in the midst of a low-density Third World War. Various world powers are fighting it out amongst themselves by proxy. Bombardment of the fabled city of Aleppo is a daily occurrence. Human casualties are a mere matter of statistics. There is crass cynicism amongst leaders of the world. I shudder to think whither we are headed.

In an instant my wandering comes back to my country. I think of human suffering caused by poverty, ignorance and corruption.

That often brings me to the last term of the UPA government at the Centre led by the Congress and headed by Dr Manmohan Singh during 2009-2014.

Manmohan Singh and I were together in the university. I happened to be a year ahead of him in MA. When he became finance minister, we felt proud of him; when he became prime minister, our pride – and hopes – grew further.

It was said that Sonia Gandhi picked him for prime ministership for his pre-eminent qualities. He would be well-behaved; he would be utterly faithful; he would not engage in any conspiracy against her.

Manmohan Singh sat in the prime ministerial chair but the seal of his office was in Sonia Gandhi's custody. Decisions were taken by her. They were coolly implemented by a servile prime minister and flunkeys placed by her under him. His ministers paid him minimum formal courtesy. His finance minister Pranab Mukherjee did not consult him in the preparation of the budget. When the 2G spectrum scam involving the telecommunication and IT minister, A. Raja, became public, all that he did was to tell his office to keep itself at an arm's length from the ministry! Amidst the mounting stink of corruption around him, the prime minister sat smugly, proud of his personal integrity. He did not seem to appreciate that a prime minister is responsible for ensuring the integrity of his government, not just preserving his own. The cabinet functions on the principle of collective responsibility.

He explained away the mess around him as something arising out of the 'compulsion of coalition'. That explanation is untenable. Coalition is an enabling provision for governance; not an alibi for misgovernance and corruption. The prime minister can't withdraw into a cocoon and wash his hands off the goings on under his watch. That makes a mockery of the parliamentary form of government.

His acceptance of a front office job became a subject of numerous jibes and jokes in the country.

His performance in the parliament was also a disappointment for all to see. He sat motionless on the front bench with both arms crossed on his chest in an unconscious gesture of self-protection while the Opposition mocked and ridiculed him and his government.

However, his worst moment was on 27 September 2013. Ajay Maken, general secretary of the Congress party, was defending the ordinance passed by the cabinet to protect convicted legislators from disqualification at a press conference. Rahul Gandhi butted in with a smug smile and dismissed the ordinance as 'nonsense', adding that it should be torn and thrown into a dustbin. Having said his piece, he walked away with a triumphant grin. At that time Manmohan Singh was flying back from his trip to the US. Innumerable people in the country believed that at such a public rebuke he would definitely resign in protest. If he had done so, he would have retrieved some of his self-respect. But he swallowed that and meekly proceeded to scrap the cabinet decision criticized by Rahul Gandhi.

My observations on Manmohan Singh may seem rather harsh for the very good and gentle person that he is. However, for a public figure – and that too the most important in the country – the standards of judgement are different and impersonal. They apply to the office-holder, not to his person. Also, the greater the pride in any person, the bigger the feeling of letdown.

His plight was made worse by the Opposition, mainly the BJP. It blocked most proceedings in the parliament and prevented the passage of some good pieces of legislation. They were paid to debate and legislate, but what they did was brawl and disrupt the functioning of the parliament. They did not fulfil their duties. The public at large witnessed a prolonged, sordid drama.

The sorry state of affairs was reflected pointedly in the clumsy manner in which the Union government handled the bifurcation of Andhra Pradesh. Having accepted the principle in 2004 and even promising it in its election manifesto of 2009, the Congress party went on delaying a decision on the matter. When, finally, it did concede Telangana on 30 July 2013, it was too late.

The discussion on the bill in the parliament and its passage showed an unprecedented low both in the conduct of members of the Congress and the tactics employed by the government. It set a new low benchmark for parliamentary conduct in India.

The result was that in the general elections which followed in April-May 2014, the Congress party was routed in Andhra Pradesh.

I saw at close quarters the two states – Andhra and Hyderabad – unite in bad faith on 1 November 1956, live in mistrust and rancour for six decades, and finally split in bitterness on 2 June 2014.

On the Nature of Political Power

Here I am tempted to proffer my theory on the decline and fall of political power.

According to Lord Acton quoted earlier, power tends to corrupt because by its nature, power is addictive. It corrupts by engendering a gradual numbness of some of the human faculties. It first attacks the sense of hearing. Men and women in power end up by being unwilling, and then unable to listen to the voice of the people.

Next, they start losing their sight. They start by ignoring the groundswell of discontent around them and end up not seeing the pointed and sharp writing on the wall.

Finally, they become dumb. They don't talk; they don't explain; they don't console people who are suffering. They don't care.

Three of their principal faculties having atrophied, they are unable to take appropriate and timely action.

At that point the situation is ripe for a revolution. The Congress party had, by its massive corruption and egregious mishandling of affairs, brought the country to that tipping point. In a democracy, the impulse for revolution is moderated by the device of periodic elections. People's yearning for change is answered by the emergence of an agent of change – a new leader.

Such a leader had been in the making in the middle rungs of the main Opposition party. He had spurned the life of a householder to steel himself in the rigour of celibacy, and dedicated himself to a mission. He had done his experiments in his own laboratory on the west coast of India. Through a series of gradual, shrewd and cunning moves he had worsted the aged leadership of his party and pitchforked himself to the forefront. He was able to ignite the minds of a committed political cadre. Hundreds of brilliant young techies from across the shores of India and from all corners of India flocked to him to offer their skills to work behind the scenes to craft a meticulous campaign strategy. So, when the moment came, the man was there to seize it. He articulated the mood of the nation though his spell-binding oratory. His juggernaut rolled on sweeping away everything before him.

The man was Narendra Modi.

Against him, the Congress party fielded an immature and inept leader in the person of Rahul Gandhi. With him in the vanguard, the battle was lost before it commenced. In May 2014 the nation hailed the new leader and gave him a mandate way beyond the forecasts of trusted psephologists.

Democracies are best sustained by simple majorities which provide for checks and balances within the system. Overwhelming majorities carry seeds of dictatorship within. But an angry, frustrated electorate, in an abandon of hope, swung to the other extreme.

The spartan prime minister started well. He jettisoned the deadwood in his party. He has not yet stopped surprising people with his innovative ideas. He has a charisma people have not seen in a leader since Nehru. His slogans of '*sab ka saath, sab ka vikaas*' – development for all ; 'Save and educate the girl child'; 'Clean India' and 'Toilet for every house' have generated enthusiasm and hope.

However, the admiration for him is mixed with a degree of apprehension caused by the statements of some of his followers. The genius of India is not revolutionary but evolutionary. Its multilayered culture is embracive and absorptive. Its ideal is as enunciated by Tagore in his poem in *Gitanjali*: 'Where the mind is without fear and the head is held high.' I hope that our march towards that Utopia will be firm and sustained.

His nemesis, however, is the Congress party, helped generally by other groups opposed to the 'hidden agenda' of BJP. Now, in power, the Modi government has adopted a number of legislative and administrative measures of the UPA which it had earlier vigorously opposed. The Congress party is now doing what BJP did to it when it was the Opposition. This cynical, petty game of settling scores makes a sickening spectacle for the public to see in the live telecast of the proceedings, specially of the Rajya Sabha. They watch the farce helplessly. Though our Constitution is based on the Westminster model, the conventions of the system which are a crucial component of that model are brazenly disregarded.

***

EPILOGUE

Oscar Wilde once said, 'All that I know, I have learnt from books – written by myself!'

This seemingly flippant remark is deeply insightful. Knowledge is crystallized only through writing. That is why they make you write compositions in school, essays in college, and theses in university.

I have often experienced that Wildean feeling earlier. What I know about the history and culture of Hyderabad is what I wrote in my books on the subject. I experienced the same feeling again when I finished writing this book. I know myself better now than I did before. In that sense it has been a cathartic experience. It has also helped me see people who affected my life in a new light.

I realize now that I have done nothing earth-shaking in my career. The scale of one's 'achievements' diminishes in the gentle retrospect of time. The inevitable and unconscious element of bias in their narration becomes apparent.

So is the case with the drama of my life straddling two centuries. I survived the great bloodbath of Partition. I was one among the first generation of men and women who served free India. I saw in flesh and blood stalwarts like Gandhi, Nehru, Patel and Azad. There were others in the second rung who were no less in terms of the sacrifices they made for the country, and in their idealism and their integrity while in power. I have had an opportunity to work with some of them.

An autobiography has intersecting circles which impinge upon the lives of others – particularly grown-up children. I plead guilty of transgressions into their lives in order to maintain the integrity of my story.

When I look back, I feel that my life has been a Bonsai tree. Bonsai is not a genetically dwarfed plant. It is a normal plant suppressed into a miniature. Yet it has all the constituents of a normal tree. So too is the case of many humans. My maternal grandmother was a tyrant. We did not have much to do with her. We had to spend a few days every winter in my grandfather's house. We saw her wrapped in a Pashmina shawl on her ornate bed with silver-clad legs. Behind her bed was an almirah which contained many treasures which we never saw. Below her bed were stocks of dried fruits and sweets of which we had a fair idea. She was always forbidding us from whatever we happened to be doing. If any child had been 'good' for the whole day by her despotic standards, she would reward him/her with a fistful of an assortment of goodies from under her bed.

Most of her children and all her grandchildren hated her.

For a long time, whenever I tried to do something, her dark ghost popped up in front of me. 'No, you can't,' it told me. I felt it pulling me back. It stayed with me before, during and after the event in question. I have not been able to fully exorcise that ghost.

There were other spectres at different stages later in my life, some of whom have been touched upon in my story.

While revising my writing I gradually came to discern a pattern in the seemingly disconnected episodes in my life. I also came to perceive their ultimate inevitability as a part of a grand design. Each one of my triumphs and setbacks were mere links in a chain which pulled me to where I stand now. I have mentioned some of these events as coincidences. Now I see my entire life as a series of coincidences over which, in the ultimate analysis, I did not have any control. A concurrence of mysterious forces made those incidents happen. That realization has generated a certain degree of acceptance and charity in my outlook.

It was for the best – it seems now – that some of the miseries and setbacks that I underwent happened when they did. I had the physical and mental strength to cope with them then. If they had happened ten or twenty years later, my old age would have been miserable.

Nostalgia

Reliving the memory of my early days in what is now Pakistan and Indian Punjab has kindled in me an acute nostalgia. I want to visit Amritsar to see the Golden Temple where I was christened over eight decades ago. I want to go to Hoshiarpur to see my college. I don't know anyone there now but still my heart craves for the winter in the countryside of the Punjab. I want to listen to unalloyed *Heer* sung by some village bard while I sit on the string cot in the field. I want to see some simple village folks dancing *Gidda* and *Bhangra*.

Why does the memory of the scent of the earth of the land of my birth ignite a bout of melancholy in me? Does it happen to every old man towards the close of his days or has the writing of this book done that to me?

*

During the course of what now seems a long life, I don't know when I contracted a terminal disease – old age.

Childhood comes and goes; youth comes and goes; but old age stays on – to take you along.

We can only look backward, not forward. So, no one can describe old age adequately except old persons. But they can't because coping with old age itself is a fulltime job. I thought I would but then I noticed some persons older still.

According to a touching saying in the south, I have seen a thousand moons. For those who have accomplished that feat, there is no mourning when they cross over. There is only celebration of their life.

***